CLASSROOM ACTIVITIES DESK BOOK FOR FUN AND LEARNING

by MURIEL SCHOENBRUN KARLIN

This is the complete guide for turning your classroom into the most exciting and stimulating learning environment possible.

Since numerous scientific studies indicate that happy, interested children are prone to higher achievement and fewer discipline problems, this remarkable book offers scores of imaginative, stimulating activities and projects geared towards making the classroom a "fun" place in which to learn.

SAVE TIME AND EFFORT!

The book will save you hours of work tracking down ideas and directions for appropriate exercises. Each activity can be conducted with common, everyday materials, and their simple step-by-step directions make them a joy to use.

In addition, virtually all the activities can be used within any subject area. For instance, you'll discover how to apply entertaining arithmetic exercises to the teaching of physical education—two subjects not usually associated with one another. It is this *uniqueness of approach* and *versatility of functions* that makes this book invaluable to teachers everywhere.

These are just some of the exciting techniques and methods you can use to bring vitality and enthusiasm to your classroom:

- **how to use enjoyable games and puzzles to teach important verbal and quantitative skills!**

- **how to utilize audio-visual "productions" to their best advantage!**

- **how to produce your students' written work in class publications!**

- **how to use over a score of fresh, creative ideas to make reading fun!**

Mail Order Sales
PARKER PUBLISHING CO., INC.
West Nyack, New York 10994

Also by the Author:

Successful Methods for Teaching the Slow Learner, Muriel S. Karlin and Regina Berger, Parker Publishing Company, Inc., 1969.

Experiential Learning: An Effective Teaching Program for Elementary Schools, Muriel S. Karlin and Regina Berger, Parker Publishing Company, Inc., 1971.

Effective Student Activities Program, Muriel S. Karlin and Regina Berger, Parker Publishing Company, Inc., 1971.

Discipline and the Disruptive Child: A Practical Guide for Elementary School Teachers, Muriel S. Karlin and Regina Berger, Parker Publishing Company, Inc., 1972.

Individualizing Instruction: A Complete Guide for Diagnosis, Planning, Teaching and Evaluation, Muriel S. Karlin and Regina Berger, Parker Publishing Company, Inc., 1973.

Administrator's Guide to a Practical Career Education Program, Muriel S. Karlin, Parker Publishing Company, Inc., 1974.

Classroom Activities Desk Book for Fun and Learning

Muriel Schoenbrun Karlin

Parker Publishing Company, Inc.

West Nyack, New York

Library of Congress Cataloging in Publication Data

Karlin, Muriel Schoenbrun.
   Classroom activities desk book for fun and learning.

   Includes index.
   1. Educational games--Handbooks, manuals, etc.
2. Creative activities and seat work--Handbooks,
manuals, etc. I. Title.
LB1029.G3K37   372.1'3   75-9705
ISBN 0-13-136358-1

Printed in the United States of America

Lovingly dedicated to
Len, Lisa, Henry, and Aline

ABOUT THE AUTHOR

MURIEL SCHOENBRUN KARLIN is a licensed principal, and is presently serving as a supervisor in the New York City School System. She has been a teacher, on both the elementary and junior high school levels, and an educational and vocational counselor, and has done extensive teacher training.

She is the author, or co-author, of nine books, including SUCCESSFUL METHODS FOR TEACHING THE SLOW LEARNER, INDIVIDUALIZING INSTRUCTION AND EXPERIMENTAL LEARNING (with Regina Berger) and AN ADMINISTRATOR'S GUIDE TO A PRACTICAL CAREER EDUCATION PROGRAM, all published by Parker Publishing Company. She is the educational consultant for Parker's Slow Learner Workshop, and editor of their Career Education Workshop. Mrs. Karlin is also a columnist, writing a weekly report on educational and vocational guidance for the Staten Island Advance. CLASSROOM ACTIVITIES DESK BOOK FOR FUN AND LEARNING is her tenth book.

The Scope and Purpose of This Book

This book will help you make learning exciting for every child. As a result, your children will learn more, because when they become enthused they will actually clamor to participate—and this participation almost guarantees greater achievement. We have really seen slow learners become avid students because they were excited by what they were doing in school.

You will also have fewer discipline problems. Children who are "with you" will be involved in your lessons. They have less time to get into mischief. We certainly are not implying that they will be quiet. Nor do we feel that a silent classroom is the only situation in which children can learn. Active, happy, interested children are far less inclined to cause problems than bored, non-motivated youngsters.

Because you, yourself, are being challenged, you will be able to actually see your teaching skills growing and developing. Your own thoughts will be stimulated, and you'll be looking for more and more ways to challenge your students. You will find, however, that your input of energy will yield far more than you expect. Ideas beget ideas.

In these pages there are probably many more ideas than you can use. Don't let the sheer quantity overwhelm you. We suggest you include as your goal at least one exciting idea per week, at the beginning of the year. Then, as the terms progress, you can add to this number if you like.

The techniques and methods described have not been divided into subject areas. This is because we have found virtually every technique can be used within any subject area. For example, doesn't it appear that arithmetic is far removed from physical activities? Yet, it isn't.

The concept of rhythms can be used to teach counting to little ones, for example. The football field is constantly being divided into fractions as the game progresses. Batting averages must be computed constantly. We hope to help you think in terms of using unusual methods for standard subjects, to come up with constant surprises—and to make school life more exciting for your students.

Remember, too, that some ideas may be old hat to you, but brand new to your children. A homemade pinhole camera is tremendously exciting to a child who has never made one before. The same is true of a crystal radio. A youngster who has never taken and developed a photograph will get more of a thrill from it than simply taking the film to a local drugstore.

You will find a broad range of methods that will help you stimulate and inspire your students. We begin with the basic premise—that learning *can* be fun and *can* be made stimulating. You will discover many unusual techniques to make it so. "Productions" which tie many aspects of work together can be used as a lead-off. The second chapter shows you how to use them. Printed publications serve as excellent motivation to bring out your pupils' best work. On-site excursions and community resources can supply many valuable learning experiences. Career education can be injected into your curriculum through activities which may affect your children's entire lives. Simulations are used to train the astronauts, and we'll show you how to use them to teach your youngsters (and delight them). By actually operating a business your boys and girls will also learn material preparing them for life.

You will find games, puzzles, and techniques for making reading fun. (Isn't one of our problems that, to date, it has so often been a terrific bore? "Run, _____ , run.") To keep our curriculum up to the minute, ecology and consumer education should be included. You'll find methods for doing this.

We believe that you'll enjoy reading this book. You'll find activities that will probably cause you to say, "I must try that, tomorrow"; and you will get teaching ideas that will excite and motivate you, and in so doing will enable you to transfer your enthusiasm to your children and make their lives, and yours, ever so much richer!

Muriel S. Karlin

ACKNOWLEDGMENTS

This book is the compilation of the ideas of many fine teachers and administrators. My sincere thanks to:

Mr. Norman H. Harris, Principal of Anning S. Prall Intermediate School, Staten Island, New York, for his constant encouragement of creativity in teaching and in administration. Mr. Joseph N. Marone, Assistant Principal, and the members of the Language Arts Department, including specifically Mr. Charles Glassman, Mr. Alexander Schanzer, and Mr. Robert Pisano.

My sister-in-law, Roberta Schoenbrun (Mrs. Arnold Schoenbrun) of Oceanside, New York, for her work in science. Her dedication is best described in this little anecdote. She was going to great lengths to find fertilized eggs to do the "egg watch" this term. (You'll read about it in Chapter 1.) She searched, literally, for miles until she found a farm where they were available. When questioned why, her answer was the clue. "I had to find the eggs this year. I just had to. I couldn't let the children down." "Why?" we asked. "Why is it so important this year?" "Because," she answered, "I had promised them Kohoutek, and you know what happened to that!"

To Mrs. Gerene Boberg, of Whitman Elementary School, Spokane, Washington, and to Mr. Ed Trotter, Maplewood Elementary School, Puyallup, Washington, for their work in career education.

To Superintendent Jerome G. Kovalcik, of the Board of Education, City of New York, for permission to reprint the consumer material, for many of the photographs, and for being a constant source of information when I needed it.

Very special thanks to author Martin Buxbaum, who writes

Table Talk, a wonderful little magazine published by the Marriott Corporation, and who has written many books. Mr. Buxbaum's article on the Declaration of Independence was the inspiration for the last chapter of this book, in which it is included.

To Mrs. Helen R. Harris, of P.S. 82, Manhattan, and Miss Regina Berger, of New York City, my thanks for all the educational background they have given me, and for the work we have done together.

I am grateful for the assistance my husband, Dr. Leonard Karlin, our daughter, Lisa, and son, Henry, have given me in the preparation of this manuscript.

Last, but most important, my sincere appreciation to the teachers and students I have been privileged to work with. I hope I have been a source of inspiration to them, as they have been to me.

M.S.K.

CONTENTS

11

10. Bringing Consumer Education to Your Children............156

*A sample curriculum . . . Food . . . Clothing . . .
Housing . . . Products and Services . . . Transportation . . . Leisure and education . . . Specialized Activities.*

11. Activities to Teach Ecology........................177

*Ecology curriculum . . . Suggested ecology
activities . . . Defining ecology . . . Instituting an Ecology Club in your class . . . How to work out problems the
children can solve . . . Cleaning up neighborhood
eyesores . . . How to study air pollution . . . How to
"do something" about mosquitoes in your area . . .
Waste not, want not . . . Recycling of newspapers and
aluminum . . . Helping children to develop a love of living
things . . . Growing things in the classroom . . . Making
a compost pile . . . Actually plant trees . . . Experimenting with solar energy . . . The oceans—the last frontier on
Earth.*

12. More than a Score of Ideas to Make Reading Fun..........197

*Visit the local and the school libraries . . . Magazine and
library corner . . . Choose exciting reading
materials . . . A period for pleasure reading . . . Form a
contributing class book club . . . Use the daily
newspapers . . . Riddles and jokes . . . Progress
cards . . . Using television scripts . . . Plays are fun to
read . . . Selecting reading materials . . . Reading
aloud . . . Encouraging children to build their own
libraries . . . Posters advertising books . . . Use your
school publications . . . Book reporting with a
difference . . . Follow the author . . . See the movie—
read the book . . . Comic books and "Mad"
magazine . . . Reading races . . . Reading to do projects.*

Classroom Activities Desk Book

for Fun and Learning

1

How to Make Learning
Exciting for Every Child

Y̶ou enter your classroom and look about you. There they are—30 or 35 human beings—filled with life. They seem to have energy bursting from the seams. Do you expect them to submerge their natural impulses and sit quietly? If you do, you'll find it hard going. It's often been said children are different nowadays, and they are! And one of the differences is this abundance of vitality. As teachers, it is certainly not our role to stifle this—to change them into docile dolls or robots sitting before us. It's up to us to use this energy—to use it for learning. And, since the world really is "so full of a number of things," this shouldn't be *too* difficult. Remember, though, that that energy exists, and make up your mind you will use it to everyone's mutual benefit, rather than deny its existence.

We said the children are different. They are different from their parents and grandparents because they have had many teachers. They have had their families, their friends and their environment. Oh, you say, but so have previous generations. That's true, but they have also had that modern miracle—television. Because, whether we like it or not, television has taught them a great deal. Without question some of it has not been for their good, but a tremendous amount has. How often do children come into first grade knowing the alphabet, and beginning to read? How often do you hear surprising words out of the mouths of babes? If our teaching is to be effective, it has to take this competitor into account. We have to make our classes exciting places in which to be—and we have to make use of the one big difference between television and the classroom. Television is an observer sport. We have to make our classrooms places where the children participate rather than observe—participate actively and happily. If we have them sitting listening to us hour after hour, they might as well be in front of the tube. We have to give them so many activities that they use their bountiful energy, and at the same time learn. It's a tall order for you, the teacher. In the pages of this book we will show you how. "You mean to tell me I have to compete with television?" you are saying, and the answer is, "Yes, exactly." As you read on, try to place yourself in your children's shoes. As you study a particular activity, ask yourself, "If I were a child, would this interest me? Would it hold me?" Remember, however, there are some children whom it is very hard to interest 100 percent of the time. But you should have activities and work which will involve your youngsters. They should be involved. Paraphrasing Barnum, "Some of them some of the time, all of them some of the time, and sometimes even all of them all of the time."

Planning your lessons this way can be a real challenge for you —one which, if you yourself become really involved in, will bring you great satisfaction. Can you believe you can actually turn your children on to education? Can you believe you can actually get children to look forward to coming to school? Honestly, you can! An example: One day, I had to get in to school early (7:30 A.M.). Near the entrance to the building, a group of children were talking excitedly. "Is Mr. Glassman here yet?" they shouted at me.

"I don't really know," I answered.

"Oh," they responded, in a rather disgusted tone. "We thought he was here."

"Why are you here so early? Mr. Glassman usually comes in at 8:30," I commented.

"Well," said one, "we're doing this unit on ghosts, and we

agreed to get here early so we would have more time to discuss it."

"Oh," said I, really surprised, "what specifically have you been talking about?"

"Well, now we're experimenting with the Ouija board. Besides that, there are these two girls who really saw lights that led them to four thousand dollars buried under a rock."

"Do you really believe that?" I questioned.

"One of the girls is in our class. It's really true. Mrs. Karlin, do you believe in extra-sensory perception?"

At this point Mr. Glassman arrived, and I was invited to continue as part of the group. The excitement was obvious. How did this highly creative teacher use it? The class wrote themes on the subjects after they had discussed them. They composed and produced a play, and they read a great deal of literature on the subject. "It's one of the most successful units I teach," Mr. Glassman said. "But it's never been quite as great as when the girl who found the money was in the class."

Not every unit can be *that* exciting, but you can put verve and life into everything you teach by looking for activities and experiences which are out of the ordinary, and in which the children can participate.

Taking into Consideration the Bright, the Average and the Slow Children

In order to make learning truly exciting for every child, you will have to make plans for each one—for the bright, the so-called average, and the slow. Let us give you an example to illustrate this: Youngsters love puzzles, but because of their varying abilities, they can't all do the same ones. If you have a crossword puzzle day—and it's a great way to teach vocabulary—you should select puzzles with words of varying difficulty. (The variety stores sell books which contain a great number of such puzzles, and you can pick and choose.) Or, while some children are doing puzzles, others can be designing them. Not every child is capable of this, but the brighter ones certainly are.

Or you can have arithmetic races, again taking into consideration the variation in ability. To have a race, prepare rexographed sheets, but have them different, according to the children's capabilities to handle them. Have from ten to twenty examples per page. Announce that the winner will get a prize, and explain that they will be working at their own ability levels. Put a time limit on the contest. You may even designate a marking committee, if you feel this is advisable.

Or you may use a team approach, pitting boys against girls, and promising prizes to the winners. Then, again using materials on the children's ability levels, have them do their arithmetic. For teaching purposes, you can announce that the contest will be held on Friday, and teach "to the contest" during the week. This is a good way to make the multiplication tables exciting. (It is hopefully becoming fashionable, once again, to teach the tables. Even if it is not, we suggest very strongly that you do make sure your youngsters learn them—for their future lives will surely prove the wisdom of this.)

Filling Your Classroom with Living Things to Watch Grow

The magnificence and the mystery of growth should be brought into your classroom. However, merely having green plants around doesn't do it. There are far better ways. For example, have the children plant and grow beans. (Soak these for two days before planting.) They grow quickly and interestingly. Bulbs such as narcissus are excellent, and have beautiful fragrant blooms. Have the children do research before planting, so the bulbs are planted properly and will grow. Other types of seeds may, of course, be used. (Try soaking any seeds before planting.)

The sweet potato offers a fine source of greenery and a fine project. We observed one teacher using the vines her children were growing for lessons in arithmetic (measurement, calculations and graphing). But it was her enthusiasm which inspired the children. Each day she'd ask, bubbling, "I wonder whose vine has grown the most. Johnny, has yours? Mary's did yesterday." She actually transferred her enthusiasm to the youngsters. They couldn't wait to measure and record the results. They asked if they could add fertilizers to the water. This was voted upon, and it was decided it would be acceptable. The fertilizers, however, had no effect whatsoever on the growth of the vines.

Classes have grown tomatoes hydroponically. One company (RM Nurseries, 23587 Los Adornos, Laguna Hills, California 92653) sells a kit for $1.98 which contains all of the ingredients necessary—they include potassium, calcium, magnesium, nitrogen, phosphorus, sulfur, and also traces of the elements iron, boron, manganese, copper, zinc and molybdenum. All of these are in powdered form, which is placed in water, and fed to the plant. It takes from 10 to 14 days for your tomato seeds to germinate. The first "crop" of tomatoes is expected in 90 days, with regular watering. These are called *Space Age Tomatoes*, and for the $1.98 one receives "enough tomato seeds to grow 100 pounds of tomatoes, a starting pot, a seven-month supply of NUTRI-NT, and advice for growing the tomatoes." This can be a very exciting experiment. How do you think your children would react? You can write for full information. We've tried it. We actually grew tomatoes!

Another experiment with living things which can be one of the most stimulating and unforgettable your children will ever see, is one which takes some time and effort on your part, but which brings fantastic results. It involves enabling the children to see chicken eggs incubated, and actually hatching. The process takes 21 days—days which can be filled with the miracle of new life. You begin by obtaining an incubator—by buying, borrowing, or constructing one. The latter is not as simple as it sounds, since besides controlling the temperature, the correct moisture level within the box must be maintained.

After you get an incubator—and you may be surprised at how easily you can borrow one from your high school science department, or from the special service departments of your school system, or even the local zoo—you then must contact a poultry farmer, and ask him to sell you some fertilized eggs. (We've been advised that calling him a month in advance is not too long a period of time.) Ask for his advice, too. Then you proceed with the hatching process.

This process requires 21 days. And how exciting you can make these in your classroom, because the eggs require attention! They must be turned three times a day, just as their mother turns them. One teacher who did this experiment, Mrs. Roberta Schoenbrun, used committees to do this. Before they turned the eggs, the room was darkened, and right after the committee turned them, they made a report in the "Egg Watch Book," indicating exactly what they saw. They also made sketches in the book. There were noticeable changes from day to day as the chicks developed. Other children were involved in checking the water level in the pan, and in watching the thermometer. The temperature was entered in the Egg Watch Book at hourly intervals. (The children were learning the skill of reading the thermometer, as well as taking part in the hatching experiment.)

Because the children were very excited by what was happening,

Hatch Drills were held. The class practiced exactly how the person who first became aware of the hatching would report it to Mrs. Schoenbrun. When the chickens were being hatched, groups were permitted to watch for five minutes at a time. You can readily see just how exciting this experiment was for fourth graders. "They haven't stopped talking about it yet, and this was months ago," the teacher reports. "Neither have I, for that matter. It really is a tremendously fascinating experience."

These are just some samples of how living things can stimulate learning. The supply of them is endless—from the live bat one boy brought in, which he had found in a field, to the praying mantis cocoon which hatched on the author's desk. (And, you know, it is illegal to kill this insect. That posed a real problem!)

Life is all around us—if we take the time and make the effort to show it to our children.

One of the author's most vivid memories is of a class examining baby white mice. These laboratory animals were born in the class-room. The seventh graders were studying the beautiful little creatures (the babies are about the size of a child's thumb), and even the girls who had been squeamish about the mice before were "ohing" and "ahing," as they held the adorable little things. Enter one lady assis-tant principal. "Would you like to hold one of our babies?" a young-ster asked her. She looked at what the child was handing her, shrieked "I hate mice" and ran out of the room. We never could educate those girls to the beauties of baby mice again. *Moral:* if you have guests, be sure they will not upset your lesson. P.S.: The author was devastated. It took her months to be able to talk to the lady.

A Mystery a Day—"We think only when we are confronted by a problem."

So much of what we do in the way of education is spoon-feeding. How often we tell our children what we want them to learn, and then expect them to regurgitate it for us. One can hardly consider this interesting or stimulating. One way to avoid this is by presenting a problem to them every day. Sometimes it may be a riddle—and they do love them. Sometimes it may be a "How does it work?" (telephone, radio, television, airplanes, rockets). Sometimes it can be a problem they will have to work on—to solve by doing research. But all of these should have one thing in common—they should cause your youngsters to think.

The so-called scientific method of reasoning—stating the problem clearly and definitely, thinking of a possible solution, testing that solution, and, if it does not solve the problem, trying another solution—can be one of the most valuable tools we can give to our youngsters.

You may find your boys and girls will, if requested to do so, suggest excellent problems on their own.

"I saw this stuff advertised on television. I thought it wouldn't work, but could we try it out?" one boy asked. The product was a glue which was supposed to support a huge amount of weight. When tried out, and the children tried it in the classroom, it didn't live up to expectations—or anywhere near them. The children wrote to the company, and received an excellent reply, seriously taking into consideration what they had written. "Was your surface really dry?" the manufacturer asked. The youngsters tried the product again, and this time, with very dry surfaces, it worked far more satisfactorily.

You can find statements in the newspapers for the children to check for truth. You can investigate the amount of pollution in your area—the white handkerchief test on the window sill is a simple method. They can determine whether prices are the same in all stores throughout your area, or whether they differ from store to store. (This is fine training for the very near future when they will be consumers. Most of them are already—but on a smaller scale.)

The idea of a problem to solve every day is one which can make life far more interesting—and can provoke thought, which is what good teaching is all about. A science book of an upper grade level can provide you with much material. And, incidentally, so can the television screen. "Are werewolfs real?" can be asked of a group of youngsters—but, please, not of little ones. Another type of problem is the kind which begins "What would you do if . . .?"

In any subject area, as you teach, try to inject this concept of inserting an unknown factor. You'll find that you, yourself, will learn a lot. We will never forget being asked by one boy, "Could we work on the problem 'When is a person legally dead?' " We never did find out why he wanted to know.

Another function this problem a day serves is that it enables our children to work on such questions as, "Why is the sky blue?" and

"How deep is the ocean?" It will teach them research skills, and the ability to think a problem through. If you feel that more time is required, then of course extend it, but don't allow the youngsters to become bored, or disinterested. Move quickly, and you will find they will, too.

Having Activities Go on All the Time

Is your classroom a place where the children are participating, or where they are getting into mischief because that abundance of energy is being wasted and used nonproductively? What can you do to utilize all that Child-Power? One way is to have activities go on all of the time. Taking a leaf from the British Open Classroom book, it is certainly possible for us to have interest areas where our children can pursue what intrigues them. Painting, working with clay, reading, using weights and measures, even doing chemical experiments (carefully outlined, of course) are all possibilities. Allow the youngsters to go to their interest corners when they have finished their work. Other areas you might find valuable are playing with animals (it is surprising how rarely many children get the opportunity to do this), typing (if you can obtain an old typewriter), and even writing and drawing on the blackboard. We are always surprised at how much children enjoy doing murals and large "art works" with varying colored chalks. "But what about Billy, who never finishes his work, and who would throw the chalk if I let him use it?" you ask. Well, first of all, give Billy a chance. Structure some assignments so that he will be able to complete them. Tell him if he wants to use the chalk that's fine, but he must abide by the class rules, and not break them. So often Billy is the child who never gets to do the "fun things" in the classroom, and turns school off. Use your on-going activities to change this.

We have found that many schools have a great deal of equipment locked up in storerooms. If this is put out and the youngsters are allowed to "play" with some of it, real learning experiences will result. Many of these setups have been sold as toys. Why not use them for both playing and education?

Create an air of busyness in your class. You can do this by increasing the pace of your activities. Have the children read, write in their notebooks, draw, write on the board, look up information in reference books, and discuss things. Don't expect single activities to hold their interest for any great length of time.

We feel that, if you have a hyperactive class, you may find doing calisthenics during the day worthwhile. (The factory workers in Japan do them during their coffee breaks. Be sure every child is permitted by his physician to do this type of physical activity, though, before instituting it.)

Activity is just what the word implies—keeping the children active. If you don't, they will do it themselves.

Reading, by the way, is definitely an activity, and many teachers have made their reading corners attractive to the children by having a small carpet and pillows in one corner, where the youngsters can sit on the floor and read. Looking at the picture books, for younger children, in similar circumstances, evokes a positive feeling for school and for the teacher. "I love to go to school," one first grader reported. "We have a red carpet." When her mother came into the room and saw the tiny space covered thusly she laughed aloud. "I thought you had wall-to-wall carpeting," she told the teacher.

"No," said the teacher, "but that part of the room is very special." And so it was.

The Ever-Changing Scene

Our lives are filled with change, and yet we have a tendency in our classrooms to take it for granted. Even such miracles as walking on the moon have become commonplace, and yet they indicate the things to come, and the things which our children should be aware of. For example, through the use of technical equipment far beyond the imagination of the average person, our nation has conducted a space exploration program which only a generation ago was expected to occur in the twenty-fifth century. Our children should be made aware of the existence of this technology, and of the entire area of space exploration. These are Space Age children, many of whose future occupations will be invovled in some way with electronics, the principle behind the technology of today. Computers, for instance, are expected to become a household word as they are used in businesses and in medicine, in law enforcement, in libraries, and even in the home.

How can you show your youngsters a computer, give them an

idea of the manner in which it works? There is usually a data-processing establishment in your area which will allow youngsters to see the computer in action. It is possible you may find the parents of some of your pupils involved in this type of work, and able to show the installation to your class.

There are so very many changes in the world of today! How many of your children have ever been aboard a 747 or even a smaller jet airplane? You probably can't take them on a flight, but they may be able to visit the planes while they are in the airport. And wouldn't it be worthwhile to have them go aboard a passenger train before they go out of existence? You can use these visits as the basis for language arts lessons—for discussion, for interviewing, for compositions. They can lead to drawing, paintings or posters. Above all, they should lead to thought.

One of the developments which may change much of our living habits is the use of atomic energy to produce electricity. Have you a plant in the area which you might take them to visit? Remember, it is essential to study and discuss the developments, the changes, as well as making the visits, if the concept of our ever-changing world is to be taught meaningfully. We are moving ahead at such a fast rate that if we don't tune our youngsters in to the changes, they'll miss them. Life is too exciting for that.

Sad but true, the blue sky we enjoy may disappear as well as the locomotive which helps to obliterate it. We have a chance in our classrooms to show how pollution can change our atmosphere to such an extent that that clear day when you can see forever may never be forthcoming. And how can we prevent this? Possibly, electrically (battery) driven cars might be one answer.

For good or bad, the world is a constantly changing scene, and your children should be encouraged to see it.

Supplying Healthy Emotional Outlets
for Children Who Need Them

"What's your bag?" is one way to phrase it. Another reference to it is a person saying he's "doing his own thing." We all need emotional outlets, and we can supply these for many of our children —within the classroom.

You have children who need status—but you can't give them

tasks to do which require great mental ability. Have an Ecology Drive, and have them stacking and packaging aluminum cans or newspapers. These can be sold, and the money earned used for trips or class parties. But you are supplying an outlet for these children, as well. Those hyperactive children who have a tendency to be all over the place —have them do just that—be all over the place. They can be your deliverymen or your monitors.

If you find your children need physical activity, a short volleyball game at the end of the day is a fine reward for work well done, and supplies an outlet for some of that physical energy. Or you may find you prefer to begin the day with it—as a reward, perhaps for the previous day's good performance. There are children who find emotional release by working with clay or paint. Your activities corner takes them into consideration. We have found a number of youngsters who love to drum. Creating drums from cereal boxes, if the real things are not available, can serve as good substitutes, and they are not quite as loud. Again, we have to get over the notion that children can sit still—when often they cannot.

If the day is a beautiful one, why not take the youngsters for a nature walk, if they are young, or a geological one if they are more sophisticated? In either event, you should tell the youngsters what to look for. You might link it up with the problem of the day. For example, "What examples of erosion can we find in our own neighborhood?" or "What trees do we find growing in the vicinity of our school?" As we take into account our growing youngsters, the realization comes to us that we should not expect them to walk in lines, two by two. This is an artificial situation. As long as they walk along, observing their environment, they learn about it, and, at the same time, have an outlet for some of their energies.

Children and adults, too, often find emotional release by hammering and sawing. Try them if possible. However, these activities can prove dangerous, and must be avoided if there are children within your class who will misuse the opportunities. Most children, however, can be taught how to use equipment, so that they enjoy it and can handle it properly.

Experimentation

How many times have we heard the words, "Are we going to do an experiment today?" As the teacher becomes more sophisticated, he or she learns that an experiment will be much more effective than a demonstration, and a demonstration more effective than a lecture. As often as you can, say, "Let's do an experiment," and then proceed. Magnets lend themselves to many experiments. Let the children have the fun of discovering which materials a magnet will attract, and which it won't. Or ask them "How can you prove gravity exists?" Try having them work with optical illusions because that's great fun. Show them one or two examples, and then ask, "Can you really believe your eyes?"

"What happens to us when we exercise?" you ask, and have your children devise the experiment to find out. Do the same with the concept, "Are the lengths of our days always the same, or do they differ?" Follow this up with "How can you tell?"

In a practical vein, ask, "How often do you think we should water our plant?" Have them devise experiments to determine the optimum conditions. Then ask, "Will our plants do better if they are watered from the top or from the bottom?" In doing an experiment of this type, teach the use of controls, so that your youngsters realize they need a basis for comparison. (Begonias, you will find, will usually illustrate the benefits of watering from the bottom of the pot.) Another experiment with plants is varying the amount of light which the plant receives, instead of the amount and location of watering.

Carry your experimentation into social studies. Map reading, for instance, can be treated in the same way. "Who can figure out the shortest distance between Vicksburg and Plattsburgh?" you ask the class, and they have to work with their maps, figuring out different routes. "How many types of apples grown in New York State can you find in the markets?" you ask the children. Or, "What animals in our zoo come from other countries, and what are those countries?"

It's fun to ask the children to get permission to boil eggs at home and in no other way will they really learn how long it takes to cook a hard boiled egg, or a soft boiled one.

Making yogurt in your classroom is not difficult, and teaches the children much about the concept of "seeding." Compare this to the seeding of the clouds when rain is needed.

You might find it fun to conduct a taste test—to see if the children can tell oleomargarine from butter. Ask the children to bring in samples of various brands of oleomargarine, and spread it on crackers. Spread butter, as well, and then allow each child blindfolded to vote on which was which. The conclusion reached can be quite interesting. Many children will discover they have a hard time differentiating.

We have tried to cite different subject areas, besides the obvious science activities, in which experimentation can make your class more interesting. Have we helped you to think of a few?

Incidentally, in every area it is very effective to use your adult vocabulary with your youngsters. Make sure you define the words they do not know. Then use them a sufficient number of times so the children have an opportunity to learn them.

Contests

Contests can add real zest to your class. There are a huge variety possible, from the old fashioned spelling bee type to the combination involving luck as well as skill, and thereby giving a chance to your less bright youngsters as well as the brainy ones to win.

Implicit in the term "contest" is the idea of a prize. One young teacher solved the problem of obtaining prizes very easily. "I go to garage sales, book fairs, and church white elephant sales," she said. "I find that even today I can buy suitable prizes for 25 cents. I've found many books for even less." Remember that every prize doesn't have to be a big one, but that some token makes life far more interesting for the winner. Another teacher used old, but perfect, copies of the *National Geographic* magazine. These became much sought after, as the year progressed. It is sometimes possible to obtain books from your principal, which were given to him as samples. Some business organizations are willing to send you samples of their products, which also are suitable for prizes. Keeping your eyes and ears open makes the quest for them fun for you, too.

The spelling bee type contest can be used for motivating children to learn facts in almost any subject area. We observed this in social studies classes, and in science classes as well. While the teaching of facts should not be our only goal, they do help children to reason and to think, because they have some of the information at their fingertips.

Then there's the contest which requires the children to make lists. "How many words can you find in CONSTANTINOPLE?" has been around for a very long time. But, remember, if a child has not done the particular activity, it's new to him. And many times youngsters enjoy repetition, as well. This type of contest can be changed to "Write a list of nouns. Longest list gets a prize. Of course you may use the diction-ary if you wish.'' This is just as effective for verbs, for adjectives and for adverbs—and it does get across the parts of speech. (If you use nouns, don't permit proper nouns. We watched one child, who could write very quickly, list every member of his class, then go on to other nouns.)

Another type of contest, which we have used quite effectively in an assembly, with 500 youngsters, is one which requires a combination of skill and luck. It consisted of a series of 25 questions which everyone answered in writing. The breakdown is as follows:

5 were out-and-out luck

5 were simple facts

5 were things which had to be figured out

5 were a bit more complicated questions

4 were current events

1 was free

Explain that this is a combination—a lucky knowledge contest. (You have no idea how excited the youngsters became at that free question. It was as if someone had given them the nicest gift.)

Except for the luck questions, select material from the curriculum the children have been studying. Separate the categories, i.e., #1 luck, #2 fact, #3 something to figure out. Here are some examples of the luck questions:

1. Pick a color. (Decide in advance, which you will accept. We usually use red, and accept any variation of it—pink, maroon, rose, etc.)

2. Select a number from 1 to 100. (Any number from 30 to 40 receives full credit.)

3. Select one of the planets.

4. Pick a state in which I (meaning the person who is asking the questions) would like to live. (Select a list of three states, and give credit for a mention of any one of them.)

5. Select a three-letter word. (Give credit for any word ending with "at").

Your arithmetical questions might include something like one of the following:

1. Add 6, 8 and 14. Subtract 12. Multiply by 3. Divide by 6.

2. What is one-half of one quarter?

3. 36 inches is to one yard as _____ feet is to one mile.

4. 100 centimeters is to one meter as_____ meters is to one kilometer.

Current events questions may prove interesting because so few of our children know who the governor of their state is, or the mayor of their city. Congressmen's and Senators' names fall in the realm of very difficult questions.

Try this kind of contest before the holidays, when a regular lesson may be difficult to get across, and have the children answer the questions with a pen. Then, have them all put their pens away, and take out pencils. They can then correct the papers, and determine the winner all together. This often heightens the excitement.

Myths and Legends

Most of us are intrigued by myths or legends, particularly if they are told well. One of the best selling literature textbooks consists entirely of them. Books such as Michener's *The Source* and *Hawaii* are composed largely of such tales. If you enjoy reading aloud, you can really get and hold your children's attention as you talk about times gone by, and people who have long ago disappeared from the earth, people who are usually the possessors of superhuman powers. As your children study different areas of the world, introduce them to the myths and legends of their peoples. To define our terms, myths are stories usually founded on some fact of nature, or an event in the early history of a people. They may involve some religious belief. Many times the word is used to refer to an imaginary person, thing or event. A legend is a story handed down from the past, which usually centers around a historic person or event, but which cannot be proved to be true. Stories about Ulysses are considered myths; stories about George Washington are legends.

Shouldn't every child enjoy meeting King Midas? Try reading such tales to your children, told in vocabulary they will comprehend easily. Discuss them afterward. This type of activity offers competition to television—for myths and legends are full of adventure and mysticism. They have come down to us from Greek and Roman times mainly because they are good stories. Their themes are universal, for they speak of dreams and reality, of the strengths and the weaknesses of man and woman. At the same time, they can be very relevant to the children's lives. Read the story of Daedalus and Icarus, for instance; then bring out the idea that sometimes parents really do know more than their children—and should be listened to.

Every nation has its myths and legends, and these, tied in with geography or history, or other work being covered, can enrich school-work tremendously. Furthermore, many of our expressions come directly from them. "Pandora's box" is just one example, "cyclops" another. This helps to build vocabulary and, at the same time, enthrall the youngsters. With all of the news about rockets and rocketry, shouldn't our children have heard of Isaac Newton and his famous apple?

Enthusiasm Is the Essential Element

If you walk into your classroom exhausted and bored with your work, this boredom will be transmitted to your children almost as if by direct wire. If, on the other hand, you are interested and enthused, that, too, is conveyed to them. And if you are truly excited, almost all of your children will pick up the excitement, and come alive.

It is far too much for anyone to be enthusiastic 100 percent of the time. It takes too much out of one, physically. But it is possible to be excited and enthused some of the time—and if you are doing something you find particularly interesting, let yourself get carried away by it. We mentioned several situations in this chapter where the teacher's excitement was particularly evident—with the hatching of the chicks, with the white mice, and with the growing of the sweet potato vines. All of these are activities which would enthuse most children, but before that will happen, you, the teacher, have to feel the enthusiasm first. You have to get it across—in these cases the miracles of life, in others the joy of learning or of creating.

The same element, enthusiasm, is needed in everything you teach, to a greater or lesser degree. As you feel it, let it come out. Let yourself burst forth with remarks such as "Wow! That's great!" or "Look at this! Isn't this wonderful?" Actually teach your children how they can show their enthusiasm—how they can express it. We've seen little ones standing, squealing "OOO ooo ooo" because they didn't know any other way to show their excitement.

Enthusiasm is highly contagious. It will travel around your classroom—perhaps so much so that you may have to hold it down a bit. We described how this was done with the Hatch Drills by Mrs. Schoenbrun. However, just because the children had to whisper doesn't mean they didn't feel excitement inside them. Don't allow some of the noise of children bubbling to frighten you. No supervisor worth his or her salt would be upset by it.

When you get home from school and are discussing the day's activities, if you have nothing worth talking about, perhaps you haven't gotten interested enough in your class or your children. If what you have to say refers to negative things only, you are cheating both yourself and the girls and boys. Find something which really catches your interest and intrigues you, and teach it. See what happens—both to you personally and to your class. Do something memorable, and you'll find you'll be as much enriched as the children.

SUMMARY

In this chapter we have listed a number of activities which will constructively utilize the abundance of energy most children have. We must take into consideration, as we plan our activities, the fact that all children are not on the same intellectual level, and we must prepare activities for the bright, for the average, and for the slow child. We suggest you fill your classroom with living things for the children to grow and watch grow—such as Space-Age tomatoes, and baby chicks. We suggest you introduce a mystery a day—a problem to solve which will make your children think. By having activities going on all the time, children do not get an opportunity to get restless or bored. The world's ever-changing scene offers you a huge number of opportunities to make school exciting. For some children, who need emotional outlets, you can supply them in such salutary ways as through an Ecology Drive, or paper sale. Bringing in experiments will entice the youngsters' attention, and hold it—if they are actually doing them. Contests of varying types are fun, and they create an aura of competition which adds to the excitement. Then, to keep the children interested, but in a more quiet manner, we suggest you read and discuss myths and legends with them.

All of these activities, and all of the activities which follow depend to a large measure on the amount of enthusiasm you put into them yourself, and the response you can engender in your children. Your enthusiasm should enable you to get the children truly involved—to turn them on to school and to education—to make it fun, and something from which they get pleasure.

2

How to Use Various Types of "Productions" to Encourage and Relate Learning Experiences in Every Subject Area

Productions are an excellent way to make learning experiences important—so that they stand out in the children's minds. Taking part in one can bring the quiet child out of his shell, and encourage the noisy one to cooperate. In this chapter we are going to outline a number of productions, which you will find useful for a variety of subject areas.

Have you thought of using a camera as a teaching technique? Or a tape recorder? You'll learn, in this chapter, how to do so. You'll find ideas for taking slides and presenting slide shows, for combining slides with music, for taping reports or conversations. Making filmstrips, movies and video-taping are discussed, as are the uses of silhouettes and pantomimes. The last section of the chapter is devoted to a full production you can use, combining music, slides, drama and commentary.

These are the modern media—applied to the classroom.

Taking Slides and Presenting Slide Shows

The camera is a vehicle which can be used for a tremendous amount of teaching. We suggest you take slides rather than photographs. Children enjoy seeing the pictures you took on your trip to Spain, or France, or wherever. However, they enjoy even more taking the slides themselves, and then using them to produce shows of their own. They may have their own cameras, or they may have to use yours—or the one owned by the school. However, if you will try to inject photography into your work, you will see its results almost immediately—at any rate, as soon as that first roll of film returns and is projected.

Our task here is to point out how slides may be used to produce a fascinating program.

For science and social studies, try "An Adventure on the Beach." (If you have a seashore anywhere nearby this is feasible and very worthwhile.) There are two ways to approach this. One is based on the wonders of nature—as we can show them in this free environment. The second is through the pollution of our beaches; this will be covered later in this chapter.

The oceans provide a limitless expanse for human enjoyment and for firsthand educational experiences. Most children, when you discuss this with them, will think of the beach in terms of their own enjoyment of it—of swimming and sunning, of playing with sand and shells. But this adventure, you'll tell them, is different.

Before the trip, you will have some preparation to do.

Teach the children how to focus the camera they will be using. This is important—if their results are to prove useful.

Divide the class into committees. Have each committee work in a particular area:

1. Bird committee.
2. Plant and animal (including insect) committee.

3. Pollution committee—to study the pollutants present.
4. Shell and rock committee.
5. The water and the wave committee.
6. The sand and shoreline committee.

Instruct each committee in regard to what it is to look for, what it is to photograph, what it is to remove and bring back to class.

Plan your trip for a time of year when the weather is pleasant. If the day arrives and it isn't sunny, postpone the trip. You'll need sunshine to take good photographs, and a trip on a lovely day can be truly memorable.

You'll need several adults—other teachers, paraprofessionals or parents—because of the obvious, ever-present dangers.

This is a good trip to combine with a picnic and enables you to do a lesson on littering on-the-spot, which can be really relevant education.

Have the children in each committee take many photos, including themselves in some of them. Do close-ups of the flora and fauna and of the coastline.

Give the children time to "run free," too, but set boundaries so no one can disappear. This should be a very liberating environment, but the children should be told in advance that when you call them together it will be time for them to begin work, observing and photographing the environment, its inhabitants and contents.

Use the slides to form the basis of a production. Have the children describe and explain each slide—and the class write a commentary. The finished product may well be shown to an assembly or at a parent evening entertainment.

Note: Injections of gaiety and levity are very worthwhile. For example, a photo of a bird flying and then a child running might lead to a comment such as "Here's a herring gull (the most commonly seen bird on the beach) flying high, and Jimmy flying low."

Of course, you'll be photographing too—why should the children have all the fun?

Tell the youngsters to take their photographs so that they can show people who couldn't go on the trip exactly what an adventure on the beach can be like.

You can find many fine books on this subject—Wm. Amos' *The Life of the Seashore*, McGraw Hill Company, New York, 1966; Harold Gaty's *Nature Is Your Guide*, E. P. Dutton & Co., Inc., New

York, 1958; Leon Hausman's *Beginners' Guide to Seashore Life*, G. P. Putnam's Sons, New York, 1949.

A production combining slides with commentary can be used in almost every subject area—from a fashion show (home economics) to foreign language (slides of objects, names in the tongue being studied). How else might you use slides with commentary effectively? Another method might be combining them with music.

Combining Slides with Music

Showing the set of slides with a musical background of recordings selected by the students allows you to teach music appreciation in an acceptable manner. As you play the various selections for the children, they can decide which slides will go well with which accompaniment. A bird gliding along to the "Skater's Waltz" can be quite effective.

Or the young people may supply their own recordings to be played as certain slides are shown.

The use of a camera can be a very satisfying medium which can involve the slow learners, and even give them a chance to shine. Use this as a means of giving them ego satisfaction.

Prints can be made from slides. So can enlargements. Although neither is inexpensive, there are some which are worth the investment, and which the children will treasure.

Taped Productions of Reports, Plays or Even Conversations

Of all the skills we teach our children, listening and speaking are two which are frequently overlooked. We almost take them for granted. Yet you can teach these skills, and far more, by using the tape recorder. This piece of equipment can prove to be an unbelievably big help to you, for it catches and holds the children's attention. Let's look into one way of using it—by making taped productions of reports the children write.

First, allow your youngsters to learn how your tape recorder or cassette player (preferable) works. Explain it to them, and then allow them to experiment with it until they feel confortable and are able to operate it.

Next, explain to them that they will be asked to prepare reports which you would like to preserve—on tape, in their own voices. Stress the need for the highest possible quality, and for accuracy both in their research and written work as well as in their speech. Allow the children to select topics they will enjoy, and for which they will be able to find information. As was suggested in the previous chapter, posing the topic as a question causes the youngster to think about it. Have each child work on the answer to a different question.

After they have done their work, have them summarize their findings in writing. Then have them prepare their oral responses. All this is done, of course, before the actual taping.

Select a youngster whose diction and delivery are good, and have him or her do the announcing. Make this a very formal production, beginning, perhaps, like this:

(Start tape recording.)

"This is November 20, 19__, and class 7-106 is about to present its production 'We Wanted to Know.' This is a program consisting of questions for which we have found the answers.

"Our first student is Mary Beth Jones."

Mary Beth speaks: "My question is 'Who really were the first Europeans to visit America?' "

Then she reads her response.

When she is finished, the announcer says, "Our next question and answer comes from Bob Smith."

Every child should have his or her own question and answer. Stress the need for excellence.

When the tape is completed, play it back. Then put it away. Take it out later in the year, and replay it. The youngsters' reactions always are, "That's not me. That can't be. That doesn't sound like me!"

You have structured the situation so that you should get quality work. Insist that each child do his or her best. You can invite parents or guests to the taping. If the results are exceptionally good, other teachers may ask to play it for their classes.

The same principle may be used in making tapes of plays, or even conversations.

In the taping of plays, you can use the recording as an additional motivational device. Preparing a play for an assembly program can be a nerve-racking experience, but the taping can really help you.

You have a number of alternatives. Choose a play or offer the youngsters a choice, or have them write a play in class. Whichever method you use, however, use one which the children can become involved in. Then have them try out for the various parts. Once a cast has been chosen, use your tape recorder to record the first reading. Then go over the tape with the children, making corrections and teaching them exactly how their lines are to be said. You may want to retape a second reading or wait and retape again after the youngsters have learned their lines. You may want to tape the actual performance, too, to play back for the children at the end of the year.

We mention tape recording conversations. This is particularly valuable if you have youngsters who do not communicate well. Many have grown up in homes where they were encouraged to keep quiet rather than express themselves. In order to do this taping, and have it prove an effective activity, the children must have a conversation prepared. They may or may not use a script, but they should at least have a listing of topics so that they do not feel inadequate.

Remember—almost every child enjoys having his own voice recorded, and you can use this factor to make productions of even simple occurrences, and to motivate the youngsters.

Making Filmstrips

Another type of production which children enjoy is making a filmstrip. This is similar to taking a roll of 35 mm. film, but when processed, you ask the processor to leave the film uncut, as a roll. Working with color film will give you attractive results. If you prefer black and white you will have to have a positive strip made from the negative. Color film, such as Kodachrome, will give you a positive strip immediately.

As with every project, you are seeking to involve the children. Begin by planning with them. Decide together what would be a good topic. You may want to present a list, and have the children choose one, or they can suggest topics to you.

This production can be used in every area. For example, in arithmetic it can be used to show fractions, or decimals. The metric system can be compared to other methods of linear measurement. Volume can be shown using two and three dimensional objects, such as a flat circle or a ball, a square or a cube.

In science, instructional filmstrips are interesting to produce—"How to make a circuit," for example, or "How to study the structure of a flower." An interesting method for the latter is to photograph the flower hour by hour to see the changes which occur as it develops.

Language arts lends itself, as does social studies, to illustrating plays or stories, poems or true incidents. These are much like a series of wax museum dioramas, but with creativity and imagination a great deal can be shown in each photo.

You can use titles for your filmstrip, or coordinate it with a tape recorded commentary. You will find your children will be quite intrigued and original in supplying either titles or dialogue. Encourage them to use their imaginations—both in the planning and in the commentary.

Famous events in history are interesting to handle in this manner. The story of Nathan Hale, for example, can be worked out relatively simply, and the schoolroom aspect appeals to the children. The signing of the Declaration of Independence, too, can be handled this way.

Safety can be taught in this manner and is a very necessary area to cover. As you work on the filmstrip, you can hammer home the need for it in the home, on the streets and in the school. Bicycle riding and safety in the streets might be the subject of one entire filmstrip, with traffic rules and the causes of accidents graphically portrayed. (This may be linked with a poster campaign, with a lesson on mapping showing dangerous intersections, one way strees, play streets, etc.).

"If I could, I'd like to be_____" can be the basis of a career oriented filmstrip. This involves obtaining the "work" clothes of various career areas—such as a nurse or a mailman, a cowboy or an artist. The challenge comes in when you try to make other occupations recognizable. For example, a teacher can be holding a piece of chalk, a salesman an order pad, a mechanic a wrench.

However, the filmstrip (and commentary) is only the medium. The topic you are teaching should have intrinsic value, itself. For instance, in doing the one of the signing of the Declaration of Independence, you can include each signer's thoughts in the commentary. Those were, of course, very troubled times. The medium provides excitement. Your children will go home bubbling. When asked,

"What did you do in school today?" they'll have something to talk about and to remember. Making a good filmstrip is a challenge. Don't expect every effort to be an exceptional success.

Movies—with Titles

In making a filmstrip each scene must be completed and meaningful in and of itself, whereas when filming movies you have the added factor of action. As you plan your movie, take this into consideration. Your script must be entirely different, with as much activity as possible injected.

Before attempting to develop a script, have your children study either movies or television programs to observe scene changes, and fading in and out. Then, too, before making a film, it is necessary to thoroughly learn the subject with which you are dealing. You can use this as a basis for many lessons. "We're going to make a film about New Amsterdam and the first Dutch settlers. We have to decide what to put into it, so as we work on this unit, be thinking about the film."

If you plan a comedy, you can use children carrying in printed titles. They can enter running, jumping, or even tumbling. They can be there at the time a scene opens or to change it.

Your children might like to construct a model of the village. The early Dutch houses of the period are interesting, and can be constructed relatively easily from cardboard. By cutting through, but not removing, the cardboard, shutters and doors are made easily. Since the houses were either red or white, or made of brick, this is not difficult to represent. Add a church and a windmill, a picket fence and, of course, a waterfront.

Next introduce some of the people, dressed in simple costumes. Have the children do research to determine what these were. Peter Stuyvesant is one of the stars of the production, and you can have tryouts to see who can best fill his shoe.

Movie making with titles offers the opportunity to teach many skills. Spelling, for example, is readily brought in, as are composition skills. You can inject drawings and painting of backgrounds. As you can see, once a project is selected, it becomes motivation for many activities.

Movies with Taped Background

Combining your movie making with taping can be done in either of two ways. You can make a silent film, with a spoken commentary or musical background—which is relatively simple to do—or you can put your film to music, or have your characters speak. The synchronization, of course, poses problems. However, these can be worked out. Of course, if you are fortunate enough to have a motion picture camera with sound, or a video-taping setup, this problem disappears.

In any type of movie making, manage to have every child participate, and if possible be on camera by himself—even if only for a short time. This is not a simple matter, but it is important, and worth your attention.

One topic for a film, with music, which you might consider is "Dances Around the World." You can allow your children to select their own dances, from our own folk dancing to rock and roll. Or you might choose the different dances which have been popular in our country—beginning with the minuet, and coming down to the present day. These topics enable you to do much teaching of physical activities. Choose very simple dances which the children will enjoy.

A sports film can be handled quite effectively—and can be fun if you put the background music in with an eye and ear to humor.

What about a film of "Science Experiments We Did This Year," presented by Class XYZ? In this film each child, or possibly small groups, can perform experiments which are photographed. Then the child does his own commentary. This is a chance for you to teach composition skills and good diction, because the children need them.

Don't expect silence while the activities are going on. You won't have it. Strive for 100 percent participation, however. Have children doing research, preparing backgrounds, obtaining or creating props. By stressing authenticity, you can make their research meaningful. A child will learn far more if he is going to make use of what he learns than if it just must become part of his background. You can inject problem-solving constantly.

Your productions can be shown to your supervisors, to the parents, and to visiting dignitaries. You will notice the pride in your children's eyes when their work is praised. We have seen productions in schools where it was essential to build up the youngsters' egos—and some of the productions were unbelievably good. By using a medium to make them permanent, the ego satisfaction can be prolonged. Another medium which can be used for this is video-taping.

Video-Taping

The video-tape recorder is a highly sophisticated piece of equipment which is similar to movies with sound in terms of the end product, but it can be used differently. This difference, particularly the instant replay, and the opportunity to redo any material which needs to be redone, makes producing a video-tape with sound far simpler than making a movie.

It will be necessary for you to learn to use the equipment, and feel comfortable with it, before you can undertake any long projects. However, this is relatively simple to do. Then you can train youngsters to use it. We have seen seventh graders get fabulous results, so we can assure you the youngsters can handle it.

Here's your chance to do a real movie or television program, and motivate the children to learn many skills because they will be putting them to use. If your school has the equipment, don't hesitate to try using it.

Again a choice of topic is important. Those suggested previously are possibilities. However, with this setup you can record far more complex productions if you so desire. If you are putting on an assembly program, video-tape it, too. The tape can be shown after the performance (something children love) and again at the end of the year. You can use it the following year to motivate other classes, too. Major school productions should also be filmed this way. Children years hence will enjoy seeing them.

Probably one of the best productions is a play your class writes or adapts itself. Allow them to work out dialogue which is natural for them. Then divide the play into scenes, and begin filming immediately. Just as they do on movie sets, rehearse a scene and then film it. This makes the memorization aspect far easier than when the entire part must be learned.

Panel shows, contests, singing and dancing—all of these may be the basis for a production.

A marionette show can be great fun when filmed. However, you would want well-made puppets, and a good script. Both require time and effort, as well as considerable talent. Dolls wired might serve as the marionettes. You can use them to depict any historical situation, any fairy tale, any legend or myth. (This is the type of thing Walt Disney did so very masterfully in "It's a Small World After All.") This selection can be used for background music.

You can make a video-tape called "19__, with Class__." Then tape record periodically, the classroom events which lend themselves to taping. If you are working on a variety of units, their culminations almost automatically become occasions for taping. Include in this type of production the parents' visits, and include yourself, too. Remember, everyone loves to see himself or herself on film. Your presence adds to the fun.

Simple productions are worthwhile, and very much less work for you. For younger children a topic such as "Our Heroes" can be the basis for an excellent program. Have each child select a hero, read about him or her, and prepare a short talk. One interesting twist is to have the youngsters say, "My hero was born in ____ . He (or she) was famous for_____ . Can you tell who this person is?" Then turn the camera on the audience—and have them make guesses, until the hero is identified, or until the time limit is exceeded.

Video-taping is really one of the modern miracles which, if available to you and your class, will enrich your lessons greatly.

Silhouettes

Stretch a sheet across the room. Place a strong light behind it, allow your children to experiment, provide an audience and, *voila*, you have silhouettes. Or set up a movie screen, project a strong light, and let your children do the rest. Many of us have enjoyed producing animals on the screens with our hands and arms. Outgrowths of this activity are fun and can encourage creativity, too. They can also be used to teach letters and sounds. Construct large letters, which can be held up with the light behind them, and allow the children to take turns holding them and pronouncing their sounds. When a letter has more than one sound, have each one pronounced.

A fun show may be held by producing a program called, "What does my hat tell you about me?" Have children in various hats silhouetted—wearing a sailor hat, a nurse's cap, a football helmet, a swim cap, a baker's high hat. Encourage the children to contribute their ideas—and hats.

Silhouettes have been used since colonial times, and this type is appropriate for projection. They can be used to show hairstyles (the men's hair then being worn long) and the clothing of the time.

This is a novelty which will capture the children's imagination. Don't forget to allow them time to experiment and to have fun.

Pantomime

Linked somewhat to silhouettes is the art of pantomime. It can be used to develop the children's abilities to express themselves without words. Charades are a form of pantomime which present a problem to the youngsters for solution. Using words with which the children are familiar makes it more fun.

Another possibility, and a good way to provide quiet physical activity for little ones, is through pantomime in unison. "Let's all be cowboys in pantomime" you tell the class. You've already explained that pantomime is absolutely silent, so that they are already aware of the medium.

Still another device is to have the children act out words you place on the board. This necessitates their reading the words and translating them into actions. It's more physical activity and fun than merely reading the words.

Of course, you can have the children act out some of the material they are reading in pantomime.

Charlie Chaplin may be considered to be a pantomimist. Viewing some of his silent films or others of his era can teach the youngsters how ideas may be communicated without the spoken word, that self-expression can take place in a variety of ways. Marcel Marceau is occasionally seen on television, and may be studied with the same idea in mind.

A Full Production Combining Music, Drama and Slides

One of the most interesting productions we witnessed combined music, drama and slides to describe the threat of pollution to the community in which it was shown, and to each individual member of it. It is an excellent production for you to use with your children.

Here is a suggested basic script for you to use. Your children should add their own ideas to it.

The program consists of a series of short vignettes, shown against a darkened stage. (This eliminates the need for elaborate scenery; furthermore, it theoretically brings the audience into the action because they use their imaginations to create the background.) A movie screen is already pulled down, but not used. Some of these vignettes have musical accompaniment. Others do not. The scenes show people polluting. One is a couple with their child driving along in a car. The audience sees three people seated on what is really a bench, but which becomes a car because of the actions of the actors. The three people are a couple and their son, a child of about six or seven. The father holds a steering wheel in his hands, and the mother appears to be looking out of the window. The child is eating. They are discussing their trip, how lovely it is—"Look at that gorgeous tree, did you ever see anything so lovely. I love this time of year when the foliage is changing." This type of comment is kept up by the mother as they drive along. Each times she makes a remark, her child opens the window and throws out a piece of litter. Once it is a banana peel, another time waxed paper. Still another is an aluminum can, etc. The mother must be aware of the child's actions, but should say nothing. At some point the father comments, "With all this driving I must be missing something." This skit is extremely funny, and yet the message comes through loud and clear. *At no point is the message spelled out—or even stated.* The audience has to draw its own conclusions.

Then the lights on the stage go out, and the movie screen is lit. A scene of one of America's National Parks, or some other spot of outstanding beauty is flashed on the screen. Suddenly the music begins, quietly at first, then louder as it progresses. (Not too loud, though. That's pollution, too.) The song which we heard used was Anita Bryant singing "America the Beautiful." As the music is played, more slides are shown of beautiful scenes, interspersed with shots of pollution from the area in which the program is being shown. Automobile "graveyards" are fine for this purpose, but so is any area which shows the ravages of man. The program we saw featured scenes taken at one of the local beaches, and these were filled with an assortment of debris. Make sure that the polluted places are recognizable as being in your community or the point of the program can be lost.

After the first stanza of the song, the music stops. Another vignette. A campfire, with young people having a party around it. The type of music being played identifies the age group. (Have your children select the records to play.) The crowd is apparently having fun, laughing and joking around. Then it's time to pack up and go home. One youngster says, "Okay, let's clean up." The others argue with her, and she loses. She reluctantly says, "But how can we do this? This place looked so nice when we got here. We've spoiled it for the next crowd." Someone counters with, "Let them look for their own clean place We found ours!" *Again, no moral is stated. It must be understood by the audience without words.*

Another part of "America the Beautiful," and more slides.

The next scene is of two young people talking. "This land must have been beautiful before anyone lived here." More slides—this time of an area which has been well cared for, and appears relatively untouched.

"I wonder if it was very different," the speaker says. Then flash on scenes of crowded city streets.

"There's something about the country that's so peaceful. We live in all this noise and clutter." Again, it is shown. (The contrasts of the scenes are very important in hammering home the point.)

"But we need houses, and cities. We need transportation." (A hectic downtown photo.) And the other person says, "But we all need peace and tranquility too. Where are we going to find it—if it all disappears?"

New scene, of men in business suits sitting around a table, obviously in conference. "Progress, gentlemen, depends on us. We human beings must take into account the needs of the generations to come. This huge airplane will be able to accommodate many more people than our present planes."

"But so often our planes are traveling half empty."

"Nevertheless we need these larger planes."

"But why?"

"For progress."

Then a discussion begins on what progress really means. Does it mean benefiting people, if it hurts our environment? Where shall we call the halt? What can we as citizens do?

Again another scene and stanza of "America the Beautiful," and the same type of slides—natural beauty against pollution in your own back yard.

The last vignette is of two people walking around in regular clothes, but with gas masks. Their conversation:

"I don't really mind wearing this thing, but I wish they'd make it more attractive."

"It certainly isn't sexy. But it's better than breathing that foul air, and having your eyes hurt all the time."

"You know, I can't remember back to when the air was clean. We used to see blue sky and white clouds and sunshine sometimes, but now I feel like it's a holiday when we do."

"I always thought air pollution was a problem for cities like London or Los Angeles, but now it's all over. It's terrible in Mexico City."

"My friends even saw air pollution in a fiord in Norway."

"Doesn't anyone care about the air we breathe? I can't understand it—doesn't Congress breathe the same air? Doesn't the President? Why should the air have been permitted to get so bad that we have to wear gas masks all the time?

"If I had my choice, I think I would want to see the sunshine more than anything else. It's been weeks since we've been able to see it."

Then a speaker faces the audience. The houselights go on, and he or she talks directly to them.

"How do you feel about this?" he asks. "Is there something we can do—any or all of us? How can we find solutions? Of course, we can stop littering. We can use biodegradable materials."

At this point, a little child runs in and asks, "What's biodegradable?" The speaker very patiently turns and explains it, aloud, then returns to the audience. "But what can we do about the air? Can we help that?"

In runs a "smarty pants" type of youngster. "We could drive electric cars." He then proceeds to explain what these are, how they operate, and why they would be both practical and impractical at the same time. The speaker listens, then returns to the audience. "Have you ever seen what the exhaust of your car's engine looks like? No? Notice it when you're trying to pull out of a snow bank. See the color of the snow all over town one or two days after it falls? How can it possibly get so black so quickly?"

This time it's an adult who runs in. "What can we do? What can we do?"

Here is the time for the strong speech. Now there are no interruptions. This is where a program should be stated. Begin it with a need for action on the part of the Congress, then on the part of the local officials, then on the part of each and every one of us. End with a stirring call for everyone to do something. You might want to conclude with the idea that we can't really "Stop the World I Want to Get Off," so we must, absolutely must, make the best of it—and leave a better world for succeeding generations.

You may want to play "America the Beautiful" again, or part of it, as a conclusion, or your speaker may get the audience to draw its own conclusion.

The outline described above has, purposely, been presented in the manner it was, so that you will be able to adopt it to fit the needs of your community. Where you have a specific problem in regard to pollution, you can stress it over and over again in your vignettes. New Jersey, for example, has oil refineries which pollute the air to such an extent that countryside along the road is completely invisible, at times. Furthermore, there are incinerators in the same area, which add gases from burning rubber and other irritants to the atmosphere.

You are certainly aware of the problems in your immediate area, and can discuss them—and better still, actually show them.

You and your children can, using this material as a basis, create your own production. It's fun to write the vignettes. You can exaggerate any of these for effect. An entire class might be shown wearing gas masks, for example. Much imagination and knowledge can go into the development of this program. For example, in the last scene, or in an added vignette, you can discuss the use of atomic energy for producing electricity.

This is not meant to be considered by the reader as a complete program, but as the beginnings of your own production of "Pollution in Our Town, U.S.A." It can lead to extensive research—about the recycling of materials, about the Alaskan pipeline, about the shortage of newsprint, about the effects on the atmosphere of the removal of trees. The subject is a very broad and comprehensive one. Studying it can lead to a real understanding of important issues—and to a very fine production for use in the assembly, for parents, and for the community as well.

(Our applause to Mr. Robert Pisano, who originated and used this unit in his Language Arts classes.)

SUMMARY

In this chapter you have read of many techniques involving the media of the seventies—media which allow us to compete with the attractive media outside the classroom. Furthermore, these involve the youngsters. They become participants, rather than observers, as they take slides and prepare the commentary for a production. They may combine their slides with music, as well. You may introduce them to their own voices through the media of tape recording. Other techniques you may wish to try are making filmstrips, or moving pictures. If your school is fortunate enough to own video-taping equipment, why not experiment with it? It is not complicated—don't let it frighten you off. Silhouettes and pantomime are suggested, too. These are simpler media, but interesting experiences for your youngsters.

The chapter concludes with a production called "Pollution in Our Town," which can be adapted to your community. It combines slides, music, drama, and commentary. It is a framework you can use to develop a program of great importance—and value. At the same time it can bring out the creativity and imagination of your students.

3

How to Produce
Every Child's Work
in Magazines, Newspapers
and Books

In this chapter you will find a number of projects any of which are suitable for use in the elementary grades. Your children will enjoy them—if you introduce them with verve and enthusiasm.

You will find ideas for producing a class magazine, or a class newspaper. These will stress the children's production of written materials, with an emphasis on creativity. The same is true of producing class comic books. However, to do this you will need several children in the class who are talented in drawing. Other projects about which you will find information include productions of a "textbook," and of a scrap book of "Our Life and Times." You'll read about projects involving the writing of children's books, and of making a class anthology of favorite stories. All of these are motivational, and can bring out a surprising amount of effort and creativity from your children.

Use samples of each project (if you have them) and stress the fact, throughout, that you believe the children are mature enough to begin a project of this type and complete it. Do not set out to have them do anything which you feel is overly ambitious, but do select work which will require effort on their parts.

Producing a Class Magazine

Many schools have magazines which contain work done by the entire student body. However, few teachers will attempt to complete a magazine with their classes, and yet it is a project which is very effective, particularly with bright and average classes. Each child, consciously or subconsciously, wants to make his mark—and if you can help him to do so, you can give the youngster ego-satisfaction and a feeling of achievement which is difficult to beat.

How would you go about doing this? Here are the actual steps you might take:

1. Find a topic the children are enthusiastic about. (With one group it was Superstitions and Customs; with another Our Favorite Jokes and Funny Stories; with a third Space Travel and the World of the Year 2500.) Help the class to choose a catchy name. Then refer to the magazine by it, rather than calling it otherwise. It assumes an identity you want it to have.

2. Discuss the topic fully. Have the children do research on it. Help them to become really involved in it. The more they are immersed in it the better.

3. Then have each child do as many different projects, relevant to the topic, as he can. Begin with a requirement that each child write a minimum of one paragraph on the topic. Then he or she may write poetry, draw or paint pictures, even take photographs, or do more writing. Or you may decide to do an entire publication of limericks, of haiku poetry, or all types of poetry.

Whatever work the children do must be corrected by you and rewritten by them until it is letter perfect. This step is essential if the publication is to be a valuable teaching tool.

4. Have the children whose penmanship is good transfer their material to rexograph masters. For those whose handwriting is not clear, have the material typed. School secretaries or paraprofessionals may do the job. If not, turn to the parents.

5. Ask the parents for volunteers to type. You may have to send home a note asking for their help, but often it is forthcoming.

6. Have the children submit ideas for covers. A good cover is very important. It may be a drawing or a design done directly on a rexograph master. It may be a class photograph of which you have many prints made, so that each child may have one.

7. Remember the work of every child must be represented. We've seen high school publications in which a school of 4,000 students had the work of 15 or 20 included in it. The purpose of such magazines is literary quality. The purpose of yours, while it must be letter perfect, is to represent the work of each child.

8. Ask for volunteers for:

(a) A literary staff, from among the children. Give them responsibility for checking the work, and for deciding which should be typed. They may even be able to help you decide which material is worthy of inclusion. (However, take into consideration the fact that some work will not be of superior quality. Accept it if need be. You know which children simply cannot do better than the piece of work submitted.)

(b) A staff of illustrators to decorate and illustrate the written work.

(c) A staff to duplicate and correlate the material.

(d) A checking committee—to go over everything to make sure it's perfect.

9. This publication may be done, in the intermediate or junior high, in any subject area, even math (short biographies of famous mathematicians, math in our daily lives, games, puzzles, graphs, are possibilities).

10. Why not a party upon publication? Authors have parties, so why not your class? Invite parents and school supervisors. Present each with a copy, and have the class president or class representative make a speech. (Incidentally, we have found the mention of the word "party" brings in offers of refreshments from the children. If not, a statement from you such as, "I'll bring the_____(mention an item,

such as soda or ice cream). Can anyone bring in cake?'' usually brings in more than enough food.

11. Present your principal with several copies of the publication. Be sure to use the school heading on the first page:

School District
School Superintendent

School Name and Number
School Principal

Class_____

Teacher_____

This is protocol, good public relations, and cannot help to impress.

12. In rexographing, prepare extra copies for next year's class. They will serve as reading material and as motivation for this activity—should you choose to do it again.

13. Be careful! It is so easy to ''rather do it myself.'' Don't! Allow your committees to do as much work as they possibly can. Children respond beautifully to responsibility. They need direction, but you will find leadership qualities develop when the necessity presents itself.

14. However, you must do the final check. Don't ever allow misspelling to go out. Check the manuscript (each and every page) before it is printed. Unless necessary, don't number your pages. Usually there is no need to, and when the magazine is assembled, if there are differences in order, it doesn't matter.

Do your checking early in the morning, after you've had a good night's sleep. This type of work requires that you be very alert.

15. Please don't be grim about this. Set a deadline—and expect to be several weeks late. Don't get upset if some children have to rewrite several times. Smile and tell them how proud they'll be when their *perfect* work is published!

16. The magazine is a cooperative venture. Encourage the children to work together on it. This aspect can be a very important lesson, in and of itself, for one of the patterns of behavior we really should stress is taking part in group work and learning to cooperate in a working situation. The committee structure lends itself to this, as does the entire nature of the project.

The Class Newspaper

Similar to the class magazine in some respects, different in others, the class newspaper offers another excellent source of motivation. You can teach many things as your class works on a paper, such as making observations and adapting existing methods to suit individual needs. "Let's study the _____," you tell the class (naming one of your local papers). "What features does it have which we can use?"

The newspaper should be a fast-moving project—with several issues planned. As with the magazine, it teaches the children to work together, and that their work must be perfect. The differences lie in the approach. Make this *newsy*. Fill it with the same type of material you would find in a regular newspaper. For example, here are some of the columns you might include:

1. School and class news. Any event that has happened to one of the children, or to the entire class is best.

If no events have happened, create one. Take a class trip out to your nearest large airport. Try to arrange beforehand to have the children talk to one of the pilots, and, if possible, show them around the airplane he flies. Or arrange a visit to a local radio or television studio. Whatever excursion you plan, have a number of children acting as reporters, ready to write it up. But select something the youngsters will want to write and read about, and will want to show to their parents.

2. Sports stories. Who are the local heroes—in the class or in the school? Suggest your children interview them, and write about them. Include young ladies as well as young men in this category.

3. Human interest stories. Mary Jane devotes Saturdays to going to the local nursing home. Have one of the other boys or girls write a human interest story about her. Johnny's dog saved him from being robbed. These are good stories.

If the children would like to, allow them to interview you, or other teachers or supervisors. Many times this type of article turns out to be eminently successful.

4. Dear Abbey, and Dear Arnie. Have two "letters and answers" columns. These can be written in response to actual letters the boys and girls submit, or the authors can make up both the questions and the answers. Lots of fun—place a box for questions at the back of the room, and give the children the opportunity to put their queries in without being observed.

5. Cartoons. It's amazing how many children enjoy doing car-

tooning. You can have all types—comic strips, single box funnies, etc. Of course, this, as everything else included in the newspaper, must be in good taste.

6. Inquiring photographer . . . but without photographs, because these are too difficult to reproduce. Work out questions which are fun and yet have some significance. "Do you believe there are such things as UFOs?" is an example. Allow the children to decide which questions they will ask.

7. Boy-of-the-month and Girl-of-the-month. You may have the class select (by voting on it) two young people to honor, by writing them up in this fasion. *Caution:* Don't let any child be hurt; handle this with great tact. Popularity contests are always dangerous, and this is no exception.

8. Movie review. Here you need the parents' cooperation. Don't send children to any movie their parents would not want them to see. Can't you just see the kids telling their mothers and fathers, "But Miss So-and-So said I have to go to see Deep XXXXX because I have to review it for the class newspaper."

9. Book reviews. Very important—because this can be a technique for encouraging your children to increase their outside reading. Here, too, be very careful about your choice of books. We recently received a complaint from the parents of an eighth grader because the class was studying *Catcher in the Rye*. Fortunately we were in the clear because our Board of Education had listed it for the eighth grade. (The language is so tame, compared with the graffiti which everyone sees, that we wondered how parents could react so strongly, but they did.)

Encourage the girls and boys doing the reviews to find books their classmates will enjoy, and then to tell them enough about the book to whet their appetites, but not to give away the entire story.

10. Record reviews. If your children are interested in records, this column can be very fine. If not, skip it.

11. Talents, hobbies, and such. If Johnny loves to design cars, have him do one just for the newspaper. Mary's poems are great—of course you would include one. Use the newspaper as an outlet for the youngsters' creativity.

12. Crossword and other puzzles. No paper is complete without them.

13. Weather report. Do this in an amusing fasion, i.e., snow —followed by little boys on sleds.

14. A calendar of events to come, including holidays.

This is a sampling, and a list of suggestions. We are sure your youngsters will come up with many more ideas.

Try for several issues. Again, follow the same basics that were listed for the magazine—every child represented, and whatever he or she does must be letter perfect. Parents often will help, if asked. Use the rexograph method, and above all try for a fun paper, which the children will enjoy.

Class Produced Comic Books

We have discovered that a surprisingly large proportion of our school population draws quite nicely. This came as quite a shock since drawing is definitely not one of our talents. If a number of your children are gifted in this direction, you may want to have them work on a comic book.

The selection of the topic for your comic book is very important, since this will motivate the entire project, and yet it must be one which is suitable. Adventure, mystery, science fiction, are some topics you might consider. It is easiest to work around a central character. Some such comic strips have been running for years—witness Little Orphan Annie. Furthermore, this is the simplest kind of thing to illustrate.

At this point you have an opportunity to have a discussion on the subject of violence, since so very many comic books are filled with it. You may wish to have the children bring in examples, and point the violence out to them. You have a chance, here, to teach moral values—something which is so necessary, and which will grow right out of your lesson. "Why is there so much violence in the world?" and "What can we do about it?" are excellent topics for discussion, because this violence refers to us as individuals, as well as to nations. The song "Let there be peace on earth, and let it begin with me" says it so well.

Back to the comic book. Have the children write the story first. We suggest you use the brainstorming technique. Work with the entire class, and let them tell their ideas as they think of them. Thought begets thought, and this is often a great way to get ideas flowing. Select your main character or characters, and talk about them. Make them seem like real people. Discuss what they like to do, to eat, to talk about. Then, when the time comes to do the dialogue, you will find it much simpler than if you start creating the story immediately without working on the development of your characters.

Your comic strip will have to be in black and white, so that you can duplicate it easily. Instead of color, use texture lines—going in one direction, crossing, or vertical and horizontal. Dots can be used, too. This use of black and white takes ingenuity, which will challenge your children, too.

Don't get overly ambitious the first time your class undertakes this. Handle it as if they were writing a short story. Cut down on verbiage, and concentrate on good dialogue. (This sounds simple—but is anything but easy.)

Use simple drawings. Have some children do backgrounds, others do figures. By having the same person do one character each time he appears, you will get better results. For those children who aren't good at drawing figures, there are many details to fill in—backgrounds and such. Also, the "coloring in" of clothing and other items can be done by those who can't draw well. Try to give some detail to every youngster.

Have your story make a point. Give the book a raison d'etre. Inject humor at some point in the book. (One wonders why they were named "comic books.")

Of course, you will rexograph the entire book, and give each child a copy. To make it attractive, have the cover done in color—using felt-tipped pens, for example. You can't print it, but, if the book is worthwhile, it certainly merits having some youngsters take the time to do a cover. If it is drawn on a rexograph stencil, and run off, then some of the youngsters can work at coloring it.

We find this project surprisingly successful with youngsters who are "turned off" as far as school is concerned. Try it and see.

A Class Produced Textbook

"A class produced textbook? Who are you kidding?" Is that what you're saying? Because, honestly, it can be done. It can be done by your class alone, or working with another class. We know because some teacher friends did just this—with two fifth grade classes studying social studies.

Select a topic which is an important part of your curriculum in any subject area. Be sure it is a broad topic, which will lend itself to a good deal of research and writing. The idea of a "Nation of Immigrants" is an example of such a topic, but the number is endless.

You would not really be able to do this with a slow class, although there is an outside chance it might work. However, with a bright or even average class, you will be amazed by the results. The project we referred to came out of the class' work. If you begin with this intention, you have a head start. Once you have selected your topic, divide your class into committees, and assign each to a series of reports. These become the nucleus for the book. An interesting twist can be added if you select a topic which can involve the knowledge of older people, since then the students can do research by interviewing their grandparents, and other relatives. "What was life in 'the old country' like?" is an example. Or, "What was life like fifty years ago?"

Your reports must be perfect, if they are to go into a book, and this will encourage excellence—for a reason.

If you choose a topic such as "Life in Ancient Greece," you will find it easy to illustrate, from such sources as the *National Geographic* and other magazines. Other types of illustrations include drawings, sketches, paintings and photographs.

Look around, in your own community, for possible topics. In our locality there is a zoo which is world famous for its snake collection. This might be used for a resource for the type of textbook we are discussing.

As with the other publications we have suggested, this one certainly deserves to be duplicated and distributed to each child. You might also try submitting it to various book publishers, since the item you are working on might be exactly what they are looking for at the particular time.

Class Produced Scrap Books (Our Life and Times)

The scrap book may be used in a large variety of ways. You can have each child collect pictures and articles and make a scrap book for his own library. In this case, have the children write a summary after each article—so that you are sure they have read it, and they get the practice of summarizing. Encourage them to include photographs and drawings if they like. You may decide to limit the scrap book to science or to other topics, if you feel this would be better for your particular children.

Since we are living in times which are definitely changing (so fast that if you blink you can miss something) we believe that working on a book showing fashions, sports, cars, and above all the prices of food and clothing, as well as current events, can be a very worthwhile project. At the end of the year tell the youngsters to wrap up these books and put them away. Ten years from now, twenty, and even fifty, they will enjoy reading them. We recently did research to determine how things had changed in the last ten years (it was our school's tenth anniversary) and we were shocked by many details. The children were quite interested, which surprised us, since ten years ago many of them were one or two or three years old.

Personal photographs added to this book will make it still more valuable to the individuals. If you do one large class book, they will add greatly to that, too. A class book, which becomes part of your personal school library, will cause your children to come back to see you many years after they graduate. Scrap books are a good activity because everyone can make one, and using newspapers, this can be done relatively cheaply. Even the slow learners can be successful, and since we must find activities for them in which they can feel they have achieved something, the scrap book becomes a good vehicle for this. It can also offer an avenue for self-expression. One young man asked if he could make his scrap book entirely of things related to cars. We agreed—for the obvious reason that this was going to be an outlet for this young man (who really did not have very much interest in school work). It became a work of art—with all sorts of fine materials in it, among the best of which were the cars the boy designed. He later went on to go into the automobile business; as he said, "I love everything about it!" He certainly found his career area, something we wish we could help every student to do.

A Photo-Album of Our School Year

We have already discussed the use of the camera as an activity which children enjoy, and which can be used to summarize the work occurring in the class. This photo album can be used to do just that. During or after every important activity, have photographs taken. Allow as many children as possible to use the camera, and to be in the photographs. Each photograph or set of photographs should be accompanied by a written explanation of the activity. Have each child write an explanation, perhaps as a homework assignment, and then select one to be used in the book. (Here, too, try to give each child a chance to have his written work represented in this book.) When you are teaching a subject such as mathematics, using three-dimensional objects gives you good photographs. Science experiments, acting out of plays or literature, and maps and diagrams supply good subjects for the camera, too.

Toward the end of the year, make a special occasion of it by inviting the parents to see the presentation of this photo album to the school. Have the students write dedications, and together decide on one. Have them dedicate it to the school in general, and present it to you in particular, as the custodian of it—so that they may return to consult it when they wish. (Would you prefer it go to the library? Because they will come back—some again and again!) Also, if you care to, have some children work up a file of negatives, so that parents who want prints can borrow them—or order them if you are willing to have the printing done. Wouldn't you like to be able to return to your elementary school and see photographs of yourself? Nostalgia in the abstract is interesting; of ourselves, even more so.

Writing Stories for Younger Children—Doing Entire Books—Concepts, Drawings and Even Music

Doing a children's book can be a very rewarding experience. There are a great many ways in which this can be done. For example, it may be done as a single book, with the entire class contributing, or books can be done in committees, or written by individual children. However, basically the same suggestions will apply.

Ask the children "Who has any children's books at home?" Many have younger brothers or sisters, and others may have kept some of their own Little Golden Books, or similar children's stories. Discuss those which are brought in with the class. Look for details such as the basic story line, and how it is developed, the characters and the background. Decide on the type of story you wish to write. Will it concern people, animals or things? (Young children enjoy the conversion of inanimate objects to people-like individuals.) Will it be a story or a series of verses? Will it have many words or relatively few? Think about these things first. Before the actual writing begins, encourage the children to study the samples, before going off on their own.

When it comes to illustrating the books, they may do them by drawing, painting, coloring, or using photographs they have cut out of magazines, or even taken themselves. The magazine photographs are fine for youngsters who cannot or do not like to draw. Colorful, attractive projects can be produced in this manner.

If your class is slow in getting ideas, you may wish to brainstorm this. Ask, "Who has an idea for a story?" and write that idea on the board. "Who else?" and another idea comes forth, and is written in front of the children. Continue this until you have a great many from which everyone can choose. Tell the youngsters to begin writing as soon as they discover a possible beginning for their stories.

We have seen classes do beautiful work on this type of project. Another aspect which may be fun, after the books are completed, is going down to the lower grades to read the books to the younger children. Most boys and girls react very well to this—particularly in the fifth and sixth grades.

We saw one very attractive book called *How Do We Cross a River?* It was done in simple verse, and mentioned bridges, tunnels, ferries, rowboats, and flatboats. The conclusion, however, was this:

> My favorite way to cross a river
> Which I think is very nice
> Is to wait for a cold cold day in the winter
> And walk across on the ice.
> Wouldn't you like to try it?
> It's fun, that's really true.
> But you have to make it snappy
> Or else your ears turn blue.

Encourage your children to "test" their books by reading them to their younger brothers and sisters.

You may wish to make a contest of this. Inform the children that the five best books will be sent to a publisher asking for their consideration. Explain to the children that this does not mean the books will be published, but it does mean they will be seen and read by editors.

Adding songs to a children's book can be great fun. By putting in the music and the words, so that the songs may be played on the piano and sung, the entire book comes alive with sound. It is not necessary to be able to write music to do this. It is far simpler to use a folk song, to which the children put their own words. We recall the use of "Yankee Doodle" in a charming book which taught the multiplication tables. This particular song is very good for use in parody because the children are so familiar with it, and because it lends itself to change. Others like

"The Farmer in the Dell" and "Pop Goes the Weasel" are good, too. Children often like to write verses, and putting them into their books in this way can really be fun. (Not to every child, however. Some will be unable to do this. In that case, encourage them to concentrate on their stories. For those who can't draw, they can use cut-out photographs. You have taken care of those who cannot "think of anything." And, if worst comes to worst, tell the youngsters they can retell some of the stories with which they are familiar, but giving them a new twist. However, watch out for that new twist. It may not be exactly what you had in mind.)

Class Anthologies of Favorite Stories

Have you ever read a story, and wanted to reread it—but have never been able to find a copy? Have you thought, "I'd love to read XYZ again, but it only appeared in one book, and I'll never be able to locate it"? If you have, then perhaps you would like to have the children select their favorite stories and have them duplicated for them. But what are they learning, you ask. Ah, watch. You announce, "We're going to make up an anthology of your favorite stories. As we read each story, read it carefully, so that you will remember it. As a further reminder, write a four or five sentence summary, so that you will be able to refer to it. But first we have to decide what makes up a good short story. Why should you want to include it?" You can then teach them the elements which go into a good short story.

One seventh and eighth grade favorite, which is very short, is called "Cemetery Path," by Leonard Ross. If you have never read it, don't miss this masterpiece. In an absolute minimum of words it creates a mood, develops a character, sets an environment, and is filled with action.

Perhaps you will want to include stories written by some of the youngsters, by the entire class, or even by yourself. If the stories are worthy of this honor, they certainly should be included.

By doing this project, you can inculcate a love of reading in some of your children, and a realization of the value of books, which the schools sometimes negate. Reading for pleasure should not be ignored. Far too often enjoyment is the last reason people read. As educators, we certainly don't want this to be true, and therefore it is up to us to change it.

SUMMARY

In this chapter you have read about a number of projects which your classes can do, and which involve their producing materials such as a class magazine or a class newspaper, comic books, textbooks or scrap books. Other possibilities include a photo album of the school year, writing books for younger children, and making up an anthology of favorite stories.

These activities require the use of duplicating machines. We have suggested the rexograph, although mimeographing could be substituted, if you have only the latter available. All of the activities can be highly motivational, if you bring to them your enthusiasm and a willingness to help each child who needs your assistance. Be lavish with your praise when you get good work and cooperative when it comes to correcting errors and perfecting the work. It is essential, though, that it be letter perfect, and that the children recognize their responsibilities. Make them feel that they are working on something very important, that it is worth their best efforts, and that they can succeed if they are willing to try.

4

How to Use
on-the-Site Experiences

No one can deny that seeing is believing, or that what we experience affects us. Yet so many of our children have such a limited number of experiences that they are hampered throughout their lives by this. We owe it to our students to make up for this deprivation, and it is with this in mind that we suggest, in this chapter, some experiences you can offer to your youngsters. Of course, where you go on trips will depend on what is available in your area. But, if you search, you will find many activities which are of real interest—both to you and to your children. As you read about these excursions, consider their appeal and what they offer experientially. Question your children. You will probably be amazed by how few have visited a zoo within the last year. Why did we select a zoo for this discussion? Because most parents will recognize the need for their young children to learn about the world and its inhabitants. Most—*but not all*.

If you teach in an urban area, ask your youngsters when they last saw a cow? a sheep? or a chicken? A real, live one. Most often teachers are jolted by the number of boys and girls who have not seen these domesticated animals.

Seeing something on television is preferable to never seeing it at all, but certainly does not compare with the actual experience. Many of us have great experiences right around us, yet don't take advantage of them. Lowell Thomas, one of the world's most traveled men, has called New York City's Empire State Building one of the seven wonders of the modern world, yet how many people living in the part of the nation near New York, and even living actually in the city, have never gone to the top to experience the view—which can be absolutely, unbelievably beautiful. Taking a class of youngsters to see it can provide them with one of the thrills of their lives. Because of the safety precautions, the visit is not in the least frightening—even for the smallest child, or the most timid.

In the same vein, but much closer to home, you can take your children on a helicopter ride. The helicopter enables the youngsters to get a fabulous overall view of your city or part of the country. Depending on the height at which the helicopter is flown, the view appears different. From relatively low altitudes it appears as if one is looking down at doll houses and their surroundings. (If you have visited Maduradam in the Netherlands the view is strikingly similar.) From higher up you get the impression of a huge geological contour map. Helicopter rides are not terribly expensive. Funds can be raised by the children, in a variety of ways, to pay for the rides, and yet this experience is one they will long talk about and remember. Of course, you need parental consent for this, and for any trip you take.

The Wonders of Nature

Then there are the wonders of nature. If you live in a part of the country which has glorious sunsets, introduce your children to them. Encourage them to view the sunset, and then try to put their reactions to it into words. Photographing sunsets can be very exciting and gratifying, too.

In Japan, people have parties to watch the full moon rising, and it is truly an occasion to commemorate, even if it does occur every 29th day. The moon's appearance varies with the seasons. If you have ever seen a real "harvest moon" glowing orange against a royal blue sky, you never forget it. Moon watching, too, may be suggested to your youngsters, as a source of wonderful entertainment. It can also be the motivation for very fine science lessons. The same is true of studying the phases of the moon—by viewing and drawing them. Even a person relatively deficient in talent can do this.

We have traveled over five thousand miles to Hawaii, drawn back again and again by two major attractions—major for us, that is. They are the erupting volcano (the so-called "drive-in volcanoes" of Hawaii Volcanoes National Park) on the "Big" Island, Hawaii; and the sunrise over a volcano crater which has been dormant for thousands of years. It is called *Haleakala* (Hawaiian word for "house of the sun") and is on the island of Maui. But sunrise, as well as sunset, can be thrilling anywhere one views it—providing it is visible, and not obscured by pollution. The same is true of the night sky, when one sees it from a place far from the lights of a city. The Milky Way provides a unique experience, as does the Pleides and even our old familiar friend, the Big Dipper.

One child, after seeing the moon rise, really viewing it for the first time, said, "I used to take the moon for granted. I'll never do that again. From now on it will be something special for me."

If you can open the eyes of your children to these and other beauties of nature which surround us, you can enrich the youngsters' lives immeasurably. How beautifully Paul Zindel showed this in *The Effect of Gamma Rays on Man-in-the-Moon Marigolds*. Use these wonders and beauties as motivation for creative writing or painting. Teachers often think of snow in this context, but far less often of the sunrise, sunset, or the moon rising. Clouds offer a very fertile field for the imagination. Nature's supply is unending, if one but becomes aware of it.

For the child who can look at a sunset and perhaps appreciate it, but who cannot express his appreciation, *don't make him write that composition*. Offer another topic. Don't cause him or her to reject the beauty because of a personal inadequacy. Instead suggest the pupil write about something he likes—his favorite time of the year, for example, or foods, sports, even television programs. But do bring to your children an appreciation of their environment. When you do this, you bring the world to them.

Building Construction

Within your community you may find construction going on. It doesn't matter whether it is home, office or commercial building. A visit to a building site can teach your youngsters a great deal, and be the basis for work in every subject area, or in any you choose. Of course, you will have to request permission of the builder to bring your class to visit.

Before visiting the site, you may want to write to the National Home Builders' Association, Washington, D. C., asking for their booklet for children. It is a fine survey of the careers involved in building, written on about a fourth grade level. It may well be a very valuable resource for you, too.

This visit, and what the children see and hear, can then be tied in with virtually every subject. Arithmetic comes to mind immediately. You can set up an almost endless number of lessons from simple addition and subtraction for the little people to more complex problem-solving for the older students. Measurements take on a far more significant aspect when taught in this context. The same is true of drawing diagrams and making scale models.

In regard to reading, the need to be able to comprehend plans, specifications and blueprints may be brought home to your students. You can use samples of these in your lessons. Vocabulary development is a natural because of the many new words the building and the men who construct it will bring to the fore. The names of tools and materials are examples of words you can utilize.

The social studies aspects of this visit are many. You can teach the need for cooperation, and for learning to work with others in harmony. Here your students will see this happening, with skilled workmen being assisted by their helpers. The need to follow safety precautions is illustrated, particularly if you visit the site of a "hard hat" job. If you wish, you can have the children draw maps of the building site in relation to other areas of the city. Your students can do research to learn about previous occupants of this section of land.

Buildings make use of many scientific principles, and these too will become more relevant if seen in operation. Take the idea of insulation, for example, and the reasons it is put into every building. Electrical systems are another aspect. The particular building materials can be discussed in terms of the advantages of some, such as brick, over others, such as wood.

Because it is extremely logical to do so, we suggest you add Career Education to the subject areas you cover as a result of this trip. Your youngsters will see many career areas in action. The construction industry utilizes many levels of workers. The helpers are semiskilled. The carpenters, plumbers, electricians and masons are skilled workers. The draftsman who drew up the plans is a technician, and the architect who designed the house is a professional. There will be other workers involved, as well. Bring every one to the attention of the children. If possible, have some of them describe their work, and discuss it with the youngsters.

(Every trip you take can become more exciting if it involves people as well as places.)

As you can see, a unit of work can easily come from this visit. You may wish to use the class newspaper as a device to tie it all together. Certainly your children can write their impressions of what they saw, and read about the building of homes from colonial times to the present. You may find some anxious to construct models of the houses they saw being built.

Taking photographs while on the trip adds to the fun, and they serve as reminders. They are also a valuable addition to the class newspaper. If you decide to do the paper, also have the children interview the people involved in the actual building.

As with every trip, if you personally visit the site without your class first, and plan the trip in detail, you can make it a more valuable experience than if you and the children visit together for the first time.

Of course, a huge office building will be more impressive to the youngsters than a small residence, but there is a great deal to be learned from either. The size of the former, of course, can make a difference in terms of being almost overwhelming. Other experiences which can have that effect are visits to a place where a bridge or tunnel is being built.

Visiting the Sites of Tunnel and Bridge Construction

The construction of a bridge or tunnel is a far more complex business than the construction of a building, and certainly worthy of a class visit. These huge enterprises can be used to teach children the tremendous amount of planning which goes on before any work can be done on the site; it can also illustrate the use of different scientific principles, many and varying types of materials, and a large number of workers in a variety of careers.

There are also special aspects to be considered. In the construction of a tunnel to carry water under New York Bay, one class went to the excavation site on the Staten Island side to observe the rock which was being dug out. It was found to be far softer than was expected, with many garnets in it. Finding the larger garnet specimens was a great thrill for the pupils, and the study of the geology growing out of this visit proved to be fascinating.

The mathematics of bridge or tunnel building can be simplified and phrased into problems the children can handle. The topic of volume is obviously tremendously important in tunnel work. Existing tunnels, too, may be added to mathematics curricula for their interest value.

In terms of science, the topic of air pressure takes on greater significance when it is related to tunnel construction. Many children have heard of "the bends" but it is far more meaningful in this context. Too often workmen are killed while working on tunnels because of their reactions to air pressure. The pressure of the water bearing down on the walls of the tunnel, and how this is counteracted, lead to interesting research. This is true, too, when the tunnel is through a mountain. There has been talk about a tunnel under the English Channel, which gives rise to many topics for study.

All of the aspects mentioned in the section on building construction apply to the tunnel and the bridge construction as well. In considering the bridge construction, other factors are evident, but materials, men and planning are specially worthy of attention. The type of bridge should be considered, and might lead to a study of the various types of bridges which engineers have designed for different localities. An interesting topic for discussion is "Galloping Gertie," the bridge which collapsed. It was located in the state of Washington.

It has been said that young engineers show interest in their future occupations while they are still in elementary schools. The visits we have suggested will enhance this interest and help to involve the youngsters further in it. For other students, it will make them more appreciative of the man-made wonders around us.

Bridge building is interesting, for another reason. American Indians often choose this type of occupation because they are able to work at great heights. This is one field in which they specialize; they often travel distances to do this work. There are few Indians living in the greater New York City area, and yet a number worked on the huge Verrazano-Narrows bridge. They came down from as far away as Buffalo.

The Living Theatre

We recently took a large group of children on a tour of New York's Lincoln Center, the city's newest entertainment complex. The tour was during the day, and there was no matinee in progress, but we were permitted to enter the Vivian Beaumont Theatre. The stage setting for *A Streetcar Named Desire* was in full view—this being a type of theatre-in-the-round, with no curtain closing it off. The youngsters were spellbound. They saw the Metropolitan Opera, and other beautiful auditoriums, but the stage setting was the thing which captivated them most. These were seventh and eighth graders, living a short distance away, and yet only a few of them had ever seen a live production of a play. How sad this is! Why should our children lose the magic which the theatre can bring? If you have the opportunity to introduce your youngsters to the living theatre, don't miss it. There is an interchange between the audience and the actors and actresses, when the play is a good one, which can be an electrifying experience. We have seen Mark Twain live, as Hal Holbrook literally becomes the famous writer and raconteur, and then seen this great actor make us believe that Abe Lincoln is alive and well and living in Illinois.

In many parts of the country, colleges are keeping the theatre alive. They deserve your support, and you will find your youngsters benefiting greatly, too, by being an audience for young would-be professional actors and actresses.

When children are studying a play, an excellent culmination for the study is seeing it produced. This is particularly true of Shakespeare, for the girls and boys will become excited as they hear words they remember, being said by actors and actresses. Seeing a production is fine preparation, too, for producing the play, or part of it, in school. Such masterpieces as *Inherit the Wind* or *The Miracle Worker* will enrich any group working on them.

Many European countries have national theatres, subsidized by their governments. Unfortunately we do not. It would be a great shame, and a loss to all of us, if our living theatre is permitted to disappear. The question of the suitability of a play which has offensive language often comes up, in terms of taking classes to see it. We feel this should be left to the parents. Many feel, as we do, that the youngsters have heard, and frequently hear, far worse in the world around them. However, before you take a group to see anything, see it yourself first—to save yourself the embarrassment if it should prove unsuitable.

If it is at all possible, and you are taking a group of children, try to arrange to have them meet some of the members of the cast. This makes the experience an even more enriching one.

Earlier in this chapter, we mentioned *The Effect of Gamma Rays*. This play is excellent for young people. So is *The Diary of Anne Frank*, or *Kiss Me Kate*, or *Oklahoma*. Give your children credit for a degree of sophistication, and don't take them to see fairy tales when they are in the sixth or seventh grades. (We know of one group who saw "The Emperor's Clothes" (as a play) and were highly indignant. Their parents might have enjoyed it—but they did not.)

Museums

We have not yet discussed visiting museums, and yet they offer a great deal of learning in a relatively short time. However, don't expect to spend two or three hours at a museum without both you and the children getting tired. Many adults find an hour a long enough period of time for actual walking.

Select the museums which offer the most to interest your children. Youngsters will generally prefer natural history to art, and science and industry to either of the others.

When a museum offers a show—in the planetarium or in an auditorium—include that in your visit. We have found that most shows—whether of slides, movies, or the so-called "sky shows"—are well received, and can make the visit easier and of longer duration for both the teacher and the children.

Visit the museum yourself, before taking a group of children, and determine, in advance, what you are going to take the children to see, and how you can make the experience worthwhile for them. Write, in advance, for the guide book or whatever publication the museum has, for this will enable you to plan more creatively. Often, too, you can obtain maps of the museum which can be duplicated for the children, if you cannot obtain enough copies from the source. Even simple brochures are a help, if you have them in advance.

Prepare your children for the visit by establishing your routines in advance, and going over them a number of times with the youngsters. You may wish to divide the class into small groups, with a leader selected by the group for each one. Then, when you have to take attendance, the group leader can do it quickly and report back to you. Head counts, without subdivisions of the class into some form of small grouping, can be onerous.

Museums offer us the opportunity to show to the children many things they have no chance to see anywhere else. The visits we take them on will whet their appetites, we hope, so that they return on their own in their spare time.

Famous Buildings and State or National Historic Sites in Your Area

It never ceases to be amazing, the number of people who have not seen sights which are in their own backyards.

The state of Oklahoma has oil wells digging below the Capital building, but how many residents of that state have never seen them? Monticello is famous as the home of Thomas Jefferson, and is architecturally magnificent, but how many school children have visited it? Thomas Alva Edison's laboratories still exist, as they were when he worked in them, but how many people living in New York or New Jersey even know they are located in West Orange, New Jersey?

You can inculcate in your children a love of traveling which will enrich their lives, by taking them to places nearby as well as far away. Check out your entire area. What is to be found that can be visited easily? Arrange for a trip as soon as you can. Then research the entire vicinity—to determine where else you can go. As has been suggested, use your trips for lessons in various subject areas, but make sure, too, that the children experience the excitement of travel and discovery.

Some time ago we took a group of children to Philadelphia, where there is a great deal to be seen. Among the places we visited —Independence Hall, the Betsy Ross house, the Franklin Institute (a fabulous museum of science and industry)—the place which made the biggest hit was the first automat. This particular restaurant has since been torn down, but the youngsters enjoyed it, and respected it for its historic significance. It certainly didn't compare, in that regard, with the Liberty Bell, but the restaurant was relevant to their lives.

Places which have been named National Historic Sites have been done so for very good reasons. Almost without exception they are worth visiting with your youngsters. In some cases, however, it is necessary to prepare the children for their visit. We found this to be true when we took a large group to Hyde Park, site of the home and library of Franklin Delano Roosevelt. Because the boys and girls had not learned enough about the four-term President, the place carried little importance for them. Even the guided tour provided by Mrs. Roosevelt, via the miracle of tape recording, did not impress them. Had they been more knowledgeable, this trip would have had far more significance.

There are National Historic Sites (also referred to as National Monuments) in all parts of the country—from Muir Woods in California (groves of magnificent redwood trees) to the Booker T. Washington birthplace in Virginia. Wherever they are, a visit to them will add interest and excitement to your teaching.

Your State Capital, and the Capital of the Nation

Every child should have a knowledge of the history of his state, and usually this is helped along by a trip to its capital city. Some are beautiful (Massachusetts' has a golden dome), some are pretentious (New York's new state buildings), some are old and a bit dusty, some are drilling for oil, but all carry with them a sense of history, and of background, which our children need.

Should you plan a trip to your state capital, arrange to have the children see the state legislature in session, if at all possible, and also to meet some of their representatives. This can bring government much closer to home, and prove valuable, too, in this regard.

If you are anywhere within easy traveling distance, we cannot urge you too strongly to see to it that your school takes its students to Washington, D.C., at some time in their early years—when the city will truly impress them. For it is a very impressive city, filled with magnificent buildings and fascinating sights. (One can easily spend hours in the Smithsonian Institute, for example, or the National Art Gallery.) As we mentioned in regard to the state capital, seeing government in action is interesting as well as educational. Prepare the children in advance, so that what they are seeing will really impress them. The Rotunda, of the Capitol Building, for instance, has been the place where many famous men have been honored, after their deaths, as they lay in state. The special subway, the huge Watergate complex (far more than what we think of when the term is mentioned), the

Kennedy Center—all of these will add to the excitement. And probably the most beautiful building of its type in the entire world awaits you —the Lincoln Memorial. We have seen even the most pseudo-sophisticated young adults react with awe as they faced Daniel Chester French's Lincoln.

You can make history and geography living and breathing subjects, rather than mere printed pages, through the use of trips and through your ability as a teacher to bring them to life.

Transportation Centers

Modern miracles all—railroad yards, seaports and airports—they are often in our midst and yet overlooked. As a teaching tool a visit to any one, or to all three, can be a motivational experience of the highest priority.

Trains

How many of your children have never ridden on a train, or been in a large railway terminal? In spite of the fact that the number of people traveling by train is far less than it was even a generation ago, a large amount of merchandise and produce is shipped by train. The amount of automation which has occurred in this industry is unbelievable. A visit to a huge terminus operated by relatively few workers is almost an emotional experience. While there are several new trains, such as the Metroliner, which travel at high speeds, most trains are aging and seem to be rather sad in appearance.

If you can take your class on a train ride, perhaps to your state capital, you may find this will be a "first" for many of your youngsters.

Seaports

Seaports are fascinating because of the huge size of the ships, and because of containerization. This manner of transport is another method new to our time, and one with which our youngsters should be familiar since it represents a coming thing. Here, too, far fewer men are employed to do the work of loading the ships than ever before. The huge containers are packed far from the docks with the merchandise to be shipped, then transported to them and put aboard. Why have containers been adopted? This is an interesting problem to pose to your students. Also, of course, ask what is the cargo being shipped, and where is its destination?

Ships are exciting! If you can arrange for a tour of a passenger liner, your youngsters will love it. Many ships permit such visits the day before sailing. There is an entrance fee, however. A visit to the engine room never fails to impress the youngsters.

Airports

Not every school is near a seaport, but the likelihood of there being an airport nearby is greater—and a visit to one should be part of the educational experience of every child. If an airport in your area has student tours, they are surely worthwhile. Even if it does not, a visit to the observation platform is a valuable experience.

Air freight has become increasingly important, and seeing planes being loaded is very interesting. So is being in the terminal, hearing plane arrivals and departures announced. In many airports it is possible, for a small fee, to listen to the radio communication between pilots and the control tower. This, too, intrigues the children.

Your students may be interested in identifying the different types of aircraft—from the relatively small helicopters which fly out of some, but not all, airports, to the huge 747s which fly internationally. Since air travel is definitely a thing of the future, isn't it incumbent upon us to bring our children closer to planes than 35,000 feet?

Geologic Sites

Geology is a branch of science which may be used to intrigue your children, and to motivate them. If you live in an area of the country which is rich in areas of geologic interest, we suggest you make use of this. For example, Los Angeles has its La Brea tar pits. A visit to them can lead into an excellent unit on prehistoric life. (Couple this with the appropriate sequence from *Fantasia* for something spectacular.)

The outstanding attractions—the Niagara Falls and the Wisconsin Dells—come to mind immediately, but these are not necessarily what we mean. (Although, they should not be ignored. If a trip to such a place can be arranged, that's wonderful!) But there are geologic places far less known—but very exciting. New Jersey's Palisades are an example. So is the part of New York State once covered with inland seas. If you have huge outcroppings of rock showing the earth's up-heaval, these will fascinate your children. Often, road building and blasting reveal such phenomena.

Reading up on the geology of your area will, we are sure, give you ideas of places to visit. Your children can be encouraged to collect specimens of rocks, too, and identify them. This hobby fascinates some youngsters, and can become an interest they pursue all of their lives.

How to Use Each Trip to the Greatest Advantage

1. No matter where you go on a trip, make it a problem-solving situation. Have the children answer questions about what they experi-ence; not only about what they see, but what they hear, smell and even touch and taste.

2. Encourage the children to react to the situations. "We'll be discussing our trip when we are back in class," you may tell them. "Notice particularly how you feel when you enter the Department of Justice for the first time. What's your reaction?" (This question elicits strange answers. We've used it when taking a group to Washington, D. C.)

3. Teach the vocabulary the children will need to know in ad-vance, so that the words they encounter are not strange to them. It's a shock to hear a child say, "I didn't know what the guide was talking about," because, of course, you did.

4. Establish your routines in advance. Decide what the young-sters are to do should they get separated from the group. Repeat the instructions several times, so that they are familiar with them.

5. Teach the background material the children will need so that they benefit from the experience.

Using Trips as Motivation

Children love trips. (So do adults, for that matter.) The idea of going somewhere can make even the most uncooperative child try a bit harder. We believe every child should be permitted to go on any class excursion. However, if you have children who do not have self-control, work with them. Speak to them, long before the trip, using the concept, "Do you want to go on our trip? You'll enjoy it. But it is not safe to take children who have no self-control. Do you think you can control your own behavior? If you can show that you are a responsible person (ask the child at this point what is meant by responsible; be sure he or she understands) then we'll be happy to have you.'' Put the responsibility on the child. Help him to realize he is the one who makes the decision—by the manner in which he shows his responsibility. Then don't expect miracles. Give the youngster a fair chance. If he does try, take him. If he doesn't, let him stay at home. Show him, if need be, that he must really be responsible for his actions. Trips can help you to bring this concept of responsibility home—and it's a very important one. You can use it again and again in your teaching.

SUMMARY

Are you interested in any of the ideas presented in this chapter? If you are–go ahead and try one or two as soon as possible. Don't wait! Your enthusiasm will fade, and your children will lose out.

A helicopter ride, for example, will thrill you–as well as your youngsters. This thrill might not extend to you if you take them to the zoo, but your girls and boys need experiences seeing animals, too.

The beauties of nature are all around us–but how lucky the children are whose teachers enable them to see these things. Sunrise, sunset, moonrise, stars, are ready for the beholder.

Back to earth, the construction sites of buildings, bridges and tunnels offer interesting excursions.

The living theatre can open a new world to some of your children, a world which transports them and enriches them.

In most areas of our country there are famous buildings, State or National Historic Sites, and museums worth visiting. The same is true of your state capital, as well as the Capitol Building, and all of Washington, D. C.

Transportation centers–rail, sea and air–offer other trips of interest, and they can be fun places, too.

Careful planning makes for better trips, as you will see if you think ahead.

Don't miss the opportunities on-the-site experiences offer. They serve as motivational devices, and also as sources of information. By giving the children questions beforehand to which they must find the answers while on the trip, you can add to its educational value. The efforts you expend, you will find, will produce excellent results because children really want to go on trips, and by taking them you are joining them, not beating them.

5

How to Teach Career Education Using Community Resources

There's a revolution in education sweeping the country. Be part of it. It's called Career Education.

First let's define it. Career Education is a concept which has many aspects. Basically, it requires every elementary teacher to develop in his or her pupils an awareness of the world of work, and of the child's place in it. In the junior high school, it involves going into depth in the specific areas in which a young person shows interest. In the senior high school, the student is given courses (in the field he chooses) which will prepare him or her for a job. (The business courses have been doing this for years.) Now it is the intent to give *every* young person skills, whether he plans to go to college or not. This is done in the tenth grade. Then in the eleventh and twelfth grades, students planning on post high school education will take courses to prepare them for that. Students going into occupations will be prepared for them.

As you can see, the thrust is for an on-going program, K through 12. For far too long our schools have really been ivory towers, almost behaving as if the world of work did not exist. Now we are changing our attitudes toward it—in terms of our children.

Many teachers have introduced career education through social studies. However, it has been suggested by the Office of Education of the Department of Health, Education and Welfare, that Career Education be given subject status of its own. Now what can you do—in your classroom—to introduce the world of work?

How to Introduce the World of Work

Try to make career education as personal and real to the child as you possibly can. We've found it highly successful to begin with statements about how "mature" this class is, and how you've found you can really discuss adult matters with them. (Why do children seem to want to be grown up ahead of themselves? Haven't you found most do?) Build on this concept of maturity—if you can find any basis at all for it. You can't lie—out and out lie—but if there is an ounce of truth in it, use it. (With older children "sophisticated" goes over in a big way.) Then go on to tell them they will be studying careers, and that this study is different because of the tremendous difference it can make in their lives. Next to choosing a husband or a wife, choosing a career is the most important decision they'll ever have to make.

In your teaching, use a people-to-people approach whenever possible. Later in this chapter we will discuss some techniques for doing this. First let's look into topics for discussion.

The units which follow are taken from *Administrator's Guide to a Practical Career Education Program*, by Muriel S. Karlin, published by Parker Publishing Company, 1974.

Our purposes are two-fold—to help the youngster develop career awareness, and to help him develop self-awareness. We seek to arouse his curiosity in regard to the working world, to encourage wholesome attitudes towards all types of work, to enlarge his occupational horizons, and to answer his questions concerning occupations.

These are the units suggested for the first and second grade:

A. There is a dignity in all work which people do—men, women, boys and girls.

B. Every boy or girl will be able to choose a career for which he or she will have to prepare.

C. It is important to find a career one enjoys. Some people have careers they like. Others do not enjoy their work.

D. What things do people need in order to live?

E. Where do people get the things they need?

F. What does the expression "earning a living" mean?

G. What do people you know do to earn their living?

H. Why should girls as well as boys prepare to earn a living?

I. How can you learn about yourself, so you can prepare for a career?

J. How will the subjects you study in school help you towards a career?

K. Why is it important that you finish jobs which you start?

In addition to these topics, it is suggested you go into detail teaching a number of careers—those in which the children show interest. You may select them from the "Career Clusters" which are outlined on the following pages. A sample of the way to handle this appears at the end of the chapter.

For grades three and four, the following units are suggested. (This is assumed those listed above have been taught. If they have not, it is recommended they be taught in grades three and four, but taught at the children's level of comprehension.)

A. The kind of work a person does affects his entire life.

B. Learning to cooperate is very important in school as well as later on, in the world of work.

C. To pick a career wisely, a person has to understand himself or herself.

D. Hobbies and interests sometimes lead to careers.

E. There are a great many careers in the area of science and/or health.

F. There are many careers which are concerned with entertainment or recreation for others.

G. We need both producers of services and producers of goods.

H. In order to be able to fill a job, a person must have certain skills.

I. There are many skills involved in working on any job. You learn a number of them in school.

J. People learn the skills they need for their careers in many different places—in high school, in college, in vocational or technical institutes, on the job, or in apprenticeships.

K. The more education and skills a person has, the more money he usually (not always) earns.

L. There are different levels of employment, depending on the skills a person has learned. Unskilled jobs require physical labor, semi-skilled people have some skills. Skilled workers have learned a number of related skills. Technical careers involve many skills, and professional jobs even more.

M. Where a person lives determines many of the careers open to him.

In these grades, too, you would go into the Career Clusters, and into careers in which your children are interested.

In grades five and six (if the children have studied the previous units) you might teach the following:

A. How can a person discover his talents?

B. What are the careers associated with language arts?

C. What careers are based on arithmetic or mathematics?

D. What careers are connected with science?

E. What are the careers associated with social studies?

F. For people talented in art or music what careers can they consider?

G. There are careers associated with health education and sports. What are they?

H. In junior and senior high school and college, you may be studying a foreign language. Which careers can this lead to?

I. What careers will you be able to select from if you find you are interested in industrial arts?

J. What careers involving home economics (and not restricted to girls) are there for us to think about?

K. Many more careers are not directly related to any one subject area than are. They use the knowledge you have learned in not one but most of your subject areas. What are some of them?

L. A large variety of careers is to be found in civic service employment—city, state or federal. What are some of them?

M. Many people prefer to be in business for themselves. They may start a business, purchase an established one, or enter a family business. This business may sell services (such as a dry cleaning store) or products (a grocery). What kinds of business are there in your community?

N. Why is it important to be happy in one's work?

O. All of your years in elementary school are preparation for your career. All of your years in high school and in college are, too. In what ways do they prepare you?

P. What happens when people are replaced by machines?

Q. Why do you think it better for a person to choose his career rather than go into it by chance?

All of these topics may be taught on any grade level—if taught so the youngsters understand and will benefit from them. Follow the curriculum, or select those topics you feel will have the most relevance, if you prefer. This material is a very short summary of various chapters of the aforementioned *Administrator's Guide to a Practical Career Education Program*. In that book a variety of activities are listed for every topic mentioned.

To make your career education teaching really vital, begin by discussing the reasons why people work.

Why Do People Work?

The concept of working, and the reasons for it, are most important. Work on this by questioning your youngsters. They usually verbalize the need to earn a living when queried about how their financial needs are met. However, they often have no idea of what food costs, and so, in covering this topic, inject the ideas of the specific expenses for food, shelter, clothing, transportation, and education. Combine this with information about salaries, and minimum wages.

There are, of course, other reasons people work. One of the most important ones is for the satisfaction it brings them, and for the interest it adds to their lives—providing they have selected an occupation for which they are suited, and which suits them. Some individuals crave excitement—and can find it in careers such as fire-fighting or law enforcement. Others want to use their creativity, and become architects or artists, actors or authors. Still other people feel a deep need to help their fellow human beings, and go into health careers or social work. In this context it is important to teach the children to recognize their personal needs.

One's career often provides intellectual stimulation, and social activity as well. If a person is challenged by the work he does, he grows intellectually because of it.

Before the "women's liberation" movement many girls had the idea that they did not need to work, that they would get married and be supported for the rest of their lives. How frequently this doesn't happen! Some girls never marry. Others are divorced, or widowed. Still others may want to add to the family income. Then, too, there are those women who are bored by being housewives and seek work outside the home. Your girls should be made aware of all of these reasons, so that they will look at the world realistically in terms of themselves.

The 15 Career Clusters

In its attempt to divide the 20,000 occupations listed in the *Dictionary of Occupational Titles* into workable units, the Office of Education came up with 15 Career Clusters, which are as follows. (They are listed alphabetically, not by the number of people earning a living in each.)

Agri-business and Natural Resources	Hospitality and Recreation
Business and Office	Manufacturing
Communication and Media	Marine Science
Construction	Marketing and Distribution
Consumer and Homemaking	Personal Service
Environment	Public Service
Fine Arts and Humanities	Transportation
Health	

How to Combine Career Education with Other Subject Areas

We have, in the past, taught some career education, usually in connection with social studies. "Our community helpers" is an example—covering the milkman, policeman, fireman, teacher, doctor, nurse, sanitation man, etc. However, as we move toward more inclusive study of Career Education, we suggest:

1. You bring into your teaching careers with which children are unfamiliar. If predictions are true, a great number of new occupations will be developed in the next forty years (the estimated working life of each person). Technology is becoming increasingly important daily —and yet where, besides on television, are our youngsters being taught about it? There are a large number of important careers as technologists which might appeal to them.

2. You use the Career Clusters as a basis for your choice of careers to cover. Of course, you would consider occupations such as office work, which will employ many of your students. However, also consider careers such as marine biologists, which are rarer, but every bit as important.

3. As you teach a subject, bring in lessons on careers. For example, as you teach a unit on weather, bring in the work of the meteorologist. When working on health, you can discuss any of the health careers—and there are many besides medicine and nursing. All varieties of technical jobs exist, for example. In mathematics you have accounting or engineering, as well as physicists and mathematicians. These are just examples. Many, many careers can be discussed as relevant parts of your lessons in subject areas.

Helping Each Child to Think About Himself or Herself in Terms of Careers

First it is necessary to get the child to realize that, in the future, perhaps 10 or 15 years, he or she will probably be working. This is very difficult for children to realize.

Secondly, develop the idea that each of us is different; each of us has different talents and interests. Discuss teaching. Ask the children what kind of person makes a good teacher—and if they think they would be happy teaching. Go into the education it requires to become a teacher, the time and financial outlay.

Go into the details of different careers. (The descriptions of actual tasks are given in great detail in the Occupational Outlook Handbook, available at your library.)

Point out that not everyone is suitable for every career. For example, a person cannot be a doctor or a dentist if he or she can't stand the sight of blood.

Make the learning relevant to the child. Bring out the fact that in order to be successful in such fields as professional sports, a person has to be very good. If one is just mediocre, his chances of success are not too good—and he should have another career in mind, a backup career, should the first choice not work out.

Encourage the youngsters to think about their strong points, and about the things which interest them. One young friend decided to become a veterinarian at the age of eight. He never wavered, and is now in a college of veterinary medicine. He seemed to have been born loving animals, and he never stopped.

Learning About Careers First-Hand, Through Interviewing and Through Speakers

Interviewing is one of the most personal of situations, and is almost unsurpassed (except for actually working on the job) for the teaching of careers. Furthermore, it contains interesting built-in features. For one thing, many children have no idea how their parents earn a living. Oh, they may know "My father is an accountant," but often haven't the slightest notion what being an accountant actually entails, on a day-to-day, task by task basis. Youngsters announce, "I want to be a television repair man" without realizing the amount of time or the training necessary. By interviewing they can learn a great deal, "right from the horse's mouth," in regard to particular careers.

To make this activity effective, have the children prepare, in class, a series of questions to be asked of the persons they are interviewing, such as the following:

1. What does your work consist of—on an hour-to-hour basis? What do you actually do?
2. Where do you work? What are the working conditions like?
3. Do you like what you are doing? Why or why not?
4. How did you decide to go into this career?
5. Where did you learn what you needed to know to go into this career?
6. Do you think a person needs particular talents or personality to succeed in this career? What are they?
7. If you had it to do over again, would you go into this career? Why or why not?

Interviewing can be done at home or in school, or while the class is on a trip. Isn't asking questions one of the best ways of learning?

Besides interviewing, speakers can give much information to your boys and girls. If the speaker is a person who wears a uniform while he works, and comes to speak in it, the children are usually quite impressed (especially the little ones). If you wish to use speakers, one very valuable source is the parents. Often you will find a wide variety of careers represented in your class.

Have the speaker talk informally for about ten minutes, and then have a question and answer period. Similar questions to those suggested for the interview may be used.

Visiting Places of Employment—Factories, Department Stores, Restaurants, Business Operations, Public and Private Institutions

Visits offer many rewards. The youngsters are placed on-the-spot, and can see, feel and smell and hear the environment. We took a group to visit an automobile assembly line. Even the eighth graders were aware of the lack of smiles on the faces of the workers. Another trip behind the scenes at a large restaurant showed the frantic pace at which most of the people there worked.

If your community is one with a large industry or two dominating it, it is worthwhile to visit the plant. Arrange for the personnel director to address the group, too, to discuss career opportunities.

Children, you will find, will observe more than you expect them to.

You can use these visits to motivate composition writing, reading, or art lessons. You can sometimes connect them with arithmetic, and always with social studies.

Visits to High Schools, Colleges, and Institutes

In terms of motivating children, visits of this kind can be highly effective, and sometimes can make a lasting impression on children. Many disadvantaged youngsters have never seen a campus, and we recall the wide-eyed admiration of a group we saw visiting Columbia University on magnificent Morningside Heights. It is not worthwhile to bombard the children with facts about course offerings, or other data; make this a fun trip for best results.

The Career Folder and Notebook

Have your children keep a career notebook and a large manila folder (envelope).

1. Encourage each child to send for information relevant to career study. (You can use this letter-writing as an activity in the teaching of language arts, for example.)

2. Another worthwhile activity is to have the children clip out stories in regard to careers from newspapers and magazines. These are easily located, and of value when you teach a particular career area. Furthermore, the girls and boys will be motivated—particularly if you give them credit for this work and allow them, on occasion, to read such articles to the class. They are valuable, too, when you wish to put up bulletin boards, or have a "Career Congress" or Occupational Fair.

3. Have the children copy notes or give them duplicated materials of the information they are given in class. You'll agree, we are sure, that the rate of forgetting is very great—and that the children should have material to which to refer.

4. It is essential that you develop the concept that the subject area of Career Education can have a tremendous effect on every student's life—and that they remember this as they study it.

How can a person discover his strong points–his talents?

Each person is "better" in one subject or activity area than another. One way a child can get some idea of his own talents is by answering the following questions:

Talent Questionnaire

1. What school subjects do I find most interesting?
2. What subjects do I find very easy?
3. What subjects do I like to read about?
4. Do I have any other abilities I could use on which to base my choice of a career?
5. If I could choose any career in the world, what would I choose?
6. What are my reasons for choosing it?
7. Do I really know what a person in that career actually does?

8. What are the actual duties?

9. Where did I learn about them?

10. Why do I think I could actually carry them out?

Encourage the children to answer as honestly as possible, pointing out this material will be of help to them later on. Also discuss the fact that any decision they make is certainly subject to change, not just once but perhaps many times.

Instruct the children to keep this questionnaire in their Career Folders. They may be surprised when they consult it in the future.

Studying Specific Careers in Detail

On every grade level, from the third up, have your children do research into careers in which they are interested. Of course, the amount of detail will vary, according to the maturity and competence of the child.

In the material which follows, the section on "the carpenter" is prepared in the manner one would expect from young children. "The pharmacist" is done by an older child, and "the policeman" by a seventh or eighth grader. You will note that each is followed by a series of activities which can be used in conjunction with the particular career. (If you were to cover "the carpenter" in grade eight, it should be done in as much detail as "the policeman" is done. If you were covering it in grade five, it should be done at approximately the level shown by the study of "the pharmacist.")

Salaries are not included here because they vary so greatly, and are affected by the year—and by the geographical area. You can get fairly accurate figures by consulting the local branch of your State Employment Service (which is really part of the United States Employment Service).

The Carpenter

What does the carpenter do when he helps to build a house?

The carpenter works with the wooden parts of a house or building. He first puts up the frame of the house, and sometimes the outside walls, if they are to be made of wood. He then puts in the long pieces of wood which will support the doors, windows, and walls.

He next adds the wood which makes up the floors. He then puts in the doors, the windows, and the studs which support the walls.

After the walls have been built, he adds the moldings, cabinets and other finishings.

What are the special things a carpenter can do?

He must work with many different kinds of tools, such as hammers, chisels, planes, drills, power tools.

The carpenter must be able to work with the other workers who help to build the house.

He stands on his feet much of the time.

He must be strong and must be able to work in many positions, such as hammering nails into wood with his hands raised over his head.

He must be able to work while standing on a ladder.

He must take pride in his work and be careful to do a good job. If he makes a mistake, it can cause many people to have to do some parts of the work over again.

How does a person learn to be a carpenter?

Some young men study carpentry in high schools. Others learn it in special schools, in apprenticeship programs (define the word carefully) or on the job.

Further Study: Activities

1. If there are any houses or other buildings being constructed in your community, or nearby, take your class to visit them. You may be able to get permission to visit the site if it is not a "hard hat" job. Explain this to the children.

2. Invite any parent or community member who is in the construction trade to speak to the children. Request he bring his tools with him, and demonstrate them.

3. If possible, arrange for the children to put together a small wooden structure by hammering nails into wood. Have each child make his own, just to get the feel of the process. (Girls as well as boys should have this opportunity.)

4. Have the children figure out how the work of one craftsman is dependent on the others, and draw a "work chain" to illustrate it.

5. Let the class develop a model of a town, with each child contributing a small building he has constructed from cardboard, construction paper, or foil.

The Pharmacist

Duties

When a person is sick, the doctor may give him or her a prescription which is taken to the drugstore, where the pharmacist (or druggist) fills it. It may have been already prepared, or the pharmacist may have to combine various drugs, depending on the instructions received from the physician.

Pharmacists also give advice to customers, and supply them with many products they need which do not require a prescription. The pharmacist is usually in charge of the drugstore, and in many cases is the owner. There are some pharmacists employed in drugstores belonging to other people as well.

There are pharmacists supervising and managing the drugstores in which they work. They are in charge of hiring and supervising store personnel, and buying whatever drugs or merchandise are needed. They oversee the general operation of the store. There are some pharmacists who only fill prescriptions, however.

Hospitals employ pharmacists, too, who also fill prescriptions and buy medical supplies. Some pharmacists are employed as medical salesmen who visit physicians and dentists, and bring to their attention new drugs which are being sold, as well as distributing samples of their company's products.

Some pharmacists teach in colleges of pharmacy, while others do research, supervise the manufacture of drugs, and help to develop new drugs.

Over 80% of pharmacists work in pharmacies, and about half of them own their own stores.

9% of pharmacists are women, and they are employed in all branches of the profession.

Special Qualifications

The pharmacist must deal with people, often sick people, so that it is necessary that he or she have patience and be able to be pleasant, even when very busy.

Since the pharmacist must follow the doctor's orders, he or she must be able to read prescriptions (which sometimes is quite difficult) in order to fill them. If a mistake is made, this could be very serious, and have a bad effect on the patient. The pharmacist must know the safe and proper quantities and dosages of drugs to give when filling prescriptions.

Most pharmacists stand almost all of their working hours.

The pharmacist must keep records, so that it is possible to tell when supplies must be ordered.

Training

In order to practice pharmacy, a person must have a license granted by the state. To obtain this, he or she must have graduated from a college of pharmacy. The complete course requires five years. The degree the person receives is either a Bachelor of Science or a Bachelor of Pharmacy.

In some states a person wishing to practice pharmacy must have a certain amount of practical experience or internship under a licensed pharmacist.

Activities

1. Arrange for the class to visit a local pharmacy. If at all possible, do so when the store is not busy. Make sure that the pharmacist has a chance to discuss his or her career with the children. Prepare for the visit in advance by working out a series of questions with the children which they may ask the pharmacist.

2. You may set up a mock pharmacy, and have the children role play. This can be fun if you have the "pharmacist" read scribbled "prescriptions." You can use product cartons and empty boxes. (Link this activity with arithmetic.)

3. Have the class prepare a panel discussion on the importance of pharmacy and the health professions, in terms of each one of us.

4. Have the children prepare a play for production on the "radio," in which they discuss all of the careers available to graduates of pharmacy college.

5. Invite a pharmaceutical representative to speak to the children about this career. (Get in touch with one of the large pharmaceutical companies to arrange this.)

6. You may wish to compare the pharmacy of today with one of the hundred years ago. As in all of the health professions, tremendous strides have been made in the development of drugs. Penicillin is only one example—there are a great many others, of course.

Police Officers

The duties of police officers are many and varied. Their job is basically to prevent criminal activities, and protect the life and property of every person. They are expected to exercise their authority whenever necessary. (This report covers policemen and policewomen employed by local governments. It does not include civilian employees of police departments; state and federal government police employees; or policemen and detectives employed by private businesses.)

The police man who works in a small community handles many police duties. In the course of a day's work, he may direct traffic at the scene of a fire, investigate a housebreaking, and give first aid to an accident victim. In a large police department, he may be given a specific task. He may be assigned to either patrol or traffic duty; smaller numbers are assigned to special work, such as accident prevention or operating communications systems. Some officers are detectives (plain-clothesmen) assigned to criminal investigation; others are experts in chemical and microscopic analysis, firearms indentification and handwriting and fingerprint identification. In very large cities, a few officers may be trained to work with special units such as mounted and motorcycle police, harbor patrols, helicopter patrols, canine corps, mobile rescue teams and youth aid services.

Policewomen work with juvenile delinquents, try to locate lost children and runaways, or search, question, book, and fingerprint women prisoners. They may also be assigned to detective squads, where they work mainly on crimes involving women.

Most newly recruited policemen begin on patrol duty, which has become particularly important as a means of preventing crime and providing other services to the public. Patrolmen may be assigned to congested business districts, outlying residential areas, or other sections of a community. They may cover their beats alone or with other patrolmen, and they may ride in a police vehicle or walk on "foot patrol." In any case, they become thoroughly familiar with conditions throughout their area and, while on patrol, remain alert for anything unusual. They note suspicious circumstances, such as open windows or lights in vacant buildings, as well as hazards to public safety such as burned-out street lights or fallen trees. Patrolmen also may watch for stolen automobiles and enforce traffic regulations. At regular intervals, they report to police headquarters through call boxes, by radio, or by walkie-talkie. They also prepare reports about their activities and may testify in court when cases result in legal action.

An estimated 330,000 full-time policemen and policewomen were employed in 1970 by local police departments. The majority were men.

Some cities have very large police forces. For example, New York has over 31,000 police officers and Chicago has over 12,000. Hundreds of small communities employ fewer than 25 policemen each. Policewomen work mainly in large cities.

Special Qualifications

Policemen and women must be particularly brave, because they must face danger whenever it arises, whether in the form of a speeding car, or a shooting criminal.

Personal qualifications include honesty, good judgment, and a sense of responsibility. Their character traits and background may be investigated. In some police departments, candidates also may be interviewed by a psychiatrist or a physchologist or given a personality test.

More and more police departments are asking their members to take courses in psychology—to help them to understand people and their problems.

Education and Training

Local civil service regulations govern the appointment of police officers in practically all large cities and in many small ones. Candidates must be U. S. citizens, usually at least 21 years of age, and be able to meet certain height and weight standards. Eligibility for appointment also is determined by performance on competitive examinations, physical and personal qualifications, and education and experience. The physical examinations often include tests of strength and agility. In large police departments, where most jobs are to be found, applicants usually must have at least a high school education. A few cities require some college training and some hire law enforcement students as police interns. Some police departments accept men who have less than a high school education as recruits, particularly if they have had work experience in a field related to law enforcement.

However, there is a trend toward requiring some college training. As a result, more than 400 colleges and universities now offer major programs in law enforcement. Other courses considered helpful in preparing for a police career include English, American history, civics and government, business law, and physics. Physical education and sports activities are especially helpful in developing the physical stamina and agility needed for police work. College training may be required for policewomen because of their specialized assignments. Training or experience in social work, teaching, or nursing is desirable.

Young men who have completed high school can enter police work in some large cities as police cadets, or trainees, while still in their teens. As paid civilian employees of the police department, they attend classes part of the time to learn police science and they also do clerical work. When police cadets who qualify in other respects reach the age of 21, they may be appointed to the police force.

Before their first assignments, policemen usually go through a period of training. In many small communities, the instruction is given informally as recruits work for about a week with experienced officers. Most extensive training, such as that provided in large city police departments, may extend over several weeks or a few months. This training includes classroom instruction in constitutional law and civil rights, as well as in state laws and local ordinances, and in the procedures to be followed in accident investigation, patrol, traffic control, and other police work. Recruits learn how to use a gun, defend themselves from attack, administer first aid, and deal with a variety of other problems.

In a large department, promotion may enable an officer to specialize in one kind of law enforcement activity such as laboratory work, traffic control, communications or work with juveniles. Promotions to the rank of sergeant, lieutenant, and captain are made according to each candidate's position on a promotion list, as determined by his performance on written examinations and his work as a police officer. Advancement opportunities generally are most numerous in large police departments, where separate bureaus work under the direction of administrative officers and their assistants.

Many types of training help police officers improve their performance on the job and prepare for advancement. Through training given at police department academies, and at colleges and other institutions, officers keep abreast of crowd-control techniques, civil defense, legal developments that affect policemen, and advances in law enforcement equipment. Many police departments encourage officers to work toward college degrees and some pay all or part of the tuition.

Employment opportunities for police officers are expected to be very favorable through the 1970's. Many new positions will arise as cities increase the size of their police forces to meet the needs of a growing population. More openings, however, will occur as policemen and policewomen retire or leave their jobs for other reasons.

Activities

1. Try to arrange for a trip to a local police department. Ask that one of the supervising officers discuss police careers with the children. Have the youngsters prepare a series of questions in regard to the various careers available.

2. Have the class write to the city (or local) and state police departments, requesting a listing of the requirements for careers in police work.

3. Photograph and newspaper display. Have children take photographs of the police on duty, and make a bulletin board of these. Collect newspaper stories of police activities to be added to this exhibit.

4. Invite a policewoman to speak to the group describing her work. If there are no policewomen employed in your area, communicate with other communities. The work of policewomen is usually quite different from that of the men, and would probably prove of interest to the children.

5. Have children write compositions describing ''The Personality of the Police Officer.'' Have these read aloud, and discussed.

SUMMARY

Career Education is the newest addition to subject areas, and can be one of the most important for your children. By adopting this program, you can really give them the background for choosing a vocation. Consideration should be given to developing the child's awareness of the world of work, and of his possible place in it. Try to make Career Education as relevant as possible, through interviews, speakers, visits to places of employment, and discussions. You can also bring it to your children within other subject areas. Introduce the 15 Career Clusters, and give illustrations of each. Teach your children why people work. Most of all, help each child to realize he will one day have to work, and that it is to his advantage to select, rather than settle, when it comes to his career.

6

How to Use Simulations
and Audio-Visual Aids
to Motivate Children
to Participate

What Is a Simulation?

"**I** guess you won't be able to go to school today, Gerry," the little boy's mother said. She fully expected to be met with shrieks of glee. Instead, Gerry became very tearful.

"But, dear, you have a temperature of 104°. You can't go to school."

"But I just have to, Mommy. We're setting off a rocket to the moon."

"You are?" Again, the mother was rather flabbergasted.

"Well, you know, it isn't exactly a real rocket, but it's exciting anyway."

"Tell me about it, Gerry," his mother queried.

"We're doing simulations," Gerry announced

100

proudly. And well he might be proud. It's a good word for a fourth grader. Then he added, "Just like they train the astronauts. Our teacher told us."

"What's a simulation?"

"It's when we make conditions as much like the real ones as possible," Gerry responded. "We have a rocket in our classroom. We made it out of cardboard boxes with chairs inside. It rests on big pieces of plywood, and we can shake it so that it really feels as if we're blasting off. Then we make the room all dark, and keep it dark while we travel to the moon. While we're going, we describe what's happening to us, and how we're feeling. It's so scary! Of course we make a real lot of noise when we blast off, and we shine a lot of red lights which get smaller and smaller as we leave the earth."

"What a sensational idea," Mrs. Johnson thought aloud. "I wonder how your teacher happened to think of it."

"Oh, I know," Gerry said. "She visited Cape Kennedy, and she saw the training the astronauts get. They have a place which is exactly like the surface of the moon, where they walk around in their space suits. Of course, they can't simulate 'No Gravity,' but they have to try."

"What happens when your rocket reaches the moon?"

Gerry grinned. "Then we show slides of the moon, and of mountains and a lunar landscape. And an astronaut walking on it."

"No wonder he wants to go to school," Mrs. Johnson realized. "I must remember to tell Dad about this."

Simulations can be as exciting and as real as you are willing to make them. They are like method acting, wherein the actor or actress is encouraged to *become* the character he is playing. Not play the actor, but become the person. Children will throw themselves into this type of activity with great verve and enthusiasm. They can learn a great deal from the experience, too. Witness our example. All sorts of relevant data regarding space travel may be brought into the unit—and yet, to the children, this is not work at all, but play.

We saw one highly creative teacher have a "campfire," in her class, with the children gathered around it. *Of course, this was an electric "fire"* from someone's fireplace, but the effect in the darkened room was fantastic. The children were telling ghost stories, each one contributing. The teacher had chosen this particular device because she had a number of children who were very poor speakers. In this situation, each child had to tell a story, for which he or she had had time to prepare. In fact, the teacher had supplied many of the stories. The effort was very successful. "I never realized just how many of the children had acting ability," she commented. "This brought it out. This was like a summer camp situation which many youngsters experience, but which most disadvantaged children do not. We even had marshmallows," she added. "They weren't toasted, but you can't have everything—and what we had, the spirit, was great."

Another simulation is excellent with foreign language classes. "You are in school in France," the teacher announces to the class studying the French language for the first time. "We will speak only in French." Then you proceed to give the children the words they need, and work with dialogue. If a monitor, or someone else comes into the room speaking English, treat this as if the person were a foreigner. The youngsters enjoy this so much! Decorate the room in the foreign language, too, with signs, drawings, etc., labeled in French.

In an entirely different vein, we used simulation in connection with science—and compassion. Some years ago we heard of the work Dr. Tom Dooley was doing, and decided to "set up a clinic" in the classroom. Several children were doctors and nurses, with white shirts on, turned around to simulate operating gowns. They "examined" the "patients," then would talk about the lack of medical supplies, and the need for help from home, since they were volunteers working in a far-off land. "We're going to run out of penicillin," one boy announced dramatically. "What can we do?" At this point a "patient" was brought in with a high fever. An infection was discovered, and much was acted out of the effect of the penicillin shortage. "*What can we do?*" The children became very involved in the simulation, and from this a fund-raising project developed, with money being sent to Dr. Dooley on several occasions for his medical missionary work. When he died, and his untimely passing was a real tragedy, the children felt a deep sense of loss. He had become very personal to them. The class had also read portions of his books, and had learned important lessons in compassion and humanity.

Teaching the Constitution and the Bill of Rights

To some people, the Bible and the Ten Commandments are followed closely by the United States Constitution and the Bill of Rights.

Yet we often neglect to teach the latter as living, important documents that gave us a freedom which was unique throughout the world. This freedom must be experienced by our children, and simulations offer one of the best ways to do this.

How can you set up such a situation? Ask for the children to decide on issues they would like to talk about. These can include such concepts as current events (while it was occurring, the Watergate investigation offered a constant source of material) or such basics as "What is really meant by freedom of speech?" It is worthwhile to note, in this connection, that the First Amendment allows a person to say anything providing it is not slanderous, does not incite people to damage property or physically harm others, or, in time of war does not endanger the nation.

Let us say that you arrange a mock television broadcast, on which one of the speakers announces, "I believe there are better governments than that of the United States. I feel that there are many people in our country who need help, but are not getting it. I want to see our government work to help these people." Is this legal? Can this person say so—to the millions of people watching television? (Get the children to really participate in this discussion. If possible get them to take sides, and get really excited about this. Experiencing free speech can be very thrilling.)

Then have the person go on to say, "I think we should mobilize. We should get guns and prepare to force Congress to act." Is this legal?

At what point does freedom cease, and danger begin—to the nation or to individuals? (Getting guns is of course inciting to riot and illegal.)

You may decide to have the children read parts of Orwell's *1984*, and then establish the situation within the classroom. "You are living under the conditions described. How would you act? How would you feel? What does privacy mean to you?" Then bring out the protection the Constitution guarantees to us, so that "Big Brother" does not watch us.

Freedom of the press is another aspect which you should bring home to your students. Again, it is based on Constitutional guarantees. Begin by having the youngsters read about John Peter Zenger. Then have them make up a paper which takes into consideration the principles brought out.

If you wish to, you can establish a "Town Hall," and allow the children to bring up their gripes about your class or your school. This takes a strong, self-assured person. If you feel you can handle it, you'll probably find that, for as many students as have negative criticisms, there will be those with positive comments. This offers a chance, too, to show the restrictions (slander, particularly) set forth by the Constitution.

If you subscribe to the doctrine that children learn best by experience rather than by other methods, this teaching technique should become one of your most important tools.

Experiencing Labor Negotiations

In our nation strikes are an important part of the national scene. They are prevented, in large measure, by labor negotiations. Yet the vast majority of the American public has no idea of what happens during the actual negotiations—and how difficult it can be to reach an agreement.

We suggest you have your class actually perform the negotiations. To prepare for this, the next time there is a strike in your community, clip all of the newspaper stories—from the first mention of the strike to the final settlement. (You may prefer to use *The New York Times* or the paper of a large city instead.) Then, when you are ready to begin the unit, you can use an actual situation, and have the children negotiate to reach a settlement.

Divide your class into two or three negotiating groups, and then divide each group into two parts. Give them as many facts as you have and let them start. By using these small groupings you can get far more student participation than if you split the class in half—and this is most worthwhile.

Encourage both sides of each group to really fight for themselves, regardless of whether they are representing labor or management. Try to get them involved. Allot a certain amount of time to the negotiations. Perhaps it may be necessary to extend them. Do so—in other words make the situation as real as you can. Don't expect a silent classroom—you won't have one if this unit is at all successful. We went into a classroom in the midst of this activity because the noise coming out of the room attracted us to it. Perhaps you may want to alert your supervisor to this, in advance.

If you find your children have no appreciation of wages because they have no idea of what it costs to live, take this up with them before beginning the unit on negotiations. One of the best ways to cover the cost of living is to have the children discuss it with their parents in terms of actual expenses. What does it cost for food? For rent, etc.? (It has been suggested, too, that you do this in connection with Career Education.) If you attempt to do labor negotiations without the children having this basic understanding, your work will be useless. It's important, too, that the children think in terms of family expenses. *A weekly salary equal to the minimum wage does not seem very little if considered in the light of a single person's expenses.*

Congressional Committees Are Fine for Simulation

Another area about which the public is rather uninformed is the functioning of various branches of the government. While many people are familiar with the meetings of the House of Representatives and of the Senate, they are not as familiar with the functionings of Congressional Committees. In order to simulate this situation, your youngsters will have to do much research. You might suggest they write to their congressmen and senators requesting information. You may question them in regard to the committees they have seen televised. While many bills have passed, there are those which have "died" in committee, and it is worthwhile to bring this out, as well.

It takes a great deal of work for a bill to become law—and if we can bring this across to our students, they will gain a new respect for it. In the course of this work, you should bring out the manner in which a person becomes chairman of a particular committee, and discuss this, too. Introduce the names of the various committees, and their areas of concern. Then have each child select a committee on which he wishes to "serve." (Limit the number of committees to four or five.) Have the oldest child in each committee serve as chairman. Each member should then prepare a possible bill, and work on it for "passage."

Step Back into History; for Instance, Have Your Class Be the Continental Congress in 1776

The play *1776* may be the basis for this simulation; either read it or see it for ideas. Don't, however, reenact the play. Instead, have each child select a person who attended the Continental Congress. (Easily done, since these are the signers of the Declaration of Independence.) Have the youngsters do research to learn about the person he or she is going to be in the simulated situation. Stress particularly what each person had to gain, and what he had to lose by signing the Declaration. Make this a personal thing. The children will learn that some of the signers had already had tragedies befall them. Others would—in the near future. Yet not one signer waivered or reneged.

Treat the situation with great solemnity and dignity. Explain, "This is far more than a play. This is a simulation. For this short time Johnny is not playing Ben Franklin. Johnny is becoming Ben Franklin."

Set the environment using felt tops for the tables and quill pens. If anyone has a chair resembling the famous one with the rising sun carved into the top of it, use that. No more props are necessary. This is an internal experience. Explain and stress its seriousness.

You may wish to do one simulation after the children have read a bit about the Constitutional Convention, and then another after they have a chance to do more research. In this way they will realize what information they must look for. (See Chapter 13 for additional background material.)

Select a Jury to Carry On the Deliberations in a Famous Case, or in a Case of Your Own

Another situation in which simulations are very effective is in studying the system of trial by jury. You may wish to use a famous case. The Scopes trial is an excellent example. However, you may also fabricate a case—or consider a famous situation. Regardless of which you decide upon, do the following:

1. Be sure each child is involved. Twelve jurors, one judge, two attorneys, take care of 15 of the children immediately. You may have several defendants or one. The rest should be witnesses.

2. Try to avoid ordinary murder trials because of the traumatic effect this might have on some of the children. However, the various defendants in the shooting of Presidents Lincoln or Kennedy might be an exception.

3. A jury is used to try many cases other than murder. Have your children look for possibilities; select some relevant to their lives.

4. A college gown makes an excellent judge's garb.

5. Emphasize the need for thorough preparation, just as lawyers must spend hours preparing their cases.

6. Review the concepts of law and justice. This activity is very effective for use during weeks before holidays because it can be made into a highly stimulating experience for the children. You may wish to combine this with a visit to your local Police Department.

Using Audio-Visual Equipment

Used with imagination, the audio-visual equipment you have can become a source of excitement and interest in your classroom. We have mentioned some of the uses in earlier chapters. In this one we will give you more ideas which you will find relatively simple, and yet quite effective. Of course, before you use any material—be it film-strip, film, tape recording or cassette—you will have previewed it first. You must really do this because you do find material you don't care to have your children see. We recall one filmstrip which was to be used in a drug abuse program. The colors were so attractive, as they simulate a drug experience, that the adults previewing it all agreed that they were intrigued, and some even said that, based on this filmstrip, they'd want to try the drug in question (LSD). This was hardly the purpose for which the filmstrip had been made—but the manufacturer had done too good a job. The production was simply too attractive, and the aim of the lesson completely destroyed.

Using Filmstrips to Bring the Children into the Work at Hand

Most teachers at one time or another use a variety of audio-visual aids. Filmstrips are probably the most popular. However, we feel they are often misused. Teachers show them, and have the children read each caption aloud. This is hardly thought-provoking. Instead, we suggest you try this method: Have a specific aim in mind. Give the youngsters a series of questions to answer. If you have a number of filmstrip projectors, and the youngsters can use the filmstrips in groups, they can stop the machine whenever they find a point they wish to jot down. If you have but one machine, show the filmstrip slowly, allowing time for note taking. Children seem to like to read aloud, but this is not a lesson in oral reading. Rather, make it one in information seeking.

There are so many filmstrips available, that you can find one for practically every topic you teach. Choose the ones you show with care—since some are far better than others.

You can also show a single frame, discuss it, and then ask the youngsters to write a composition about it. Truthfully, the drug filmstrip had such frames in it. (We did not use them, though. We had returned the filmstrip to the company posthaste.) We observed an excellent art teacher show a filmstrip of paintings with which most adults are instantly familiar (*Mona Lisa*, Van Gogh's *Sunflowers*, Rembrandt's *Night Watch*). There were twenty frames of paintings and sculpture (*Winged Victory, Venus*) and the children were to select the one they liked best, and give their reasons. The filmstrip was shown about ten times, because the children asked for it. Their papers reflected their enjoyment. *Sunflowers* won the popularity contest because the youngsters loved the bright colors.

We mention the use of the filmstrip to provide a moonscape. It can be used in like manner to provide many backgrounds, and these are far more readily available than if they had to be drawn or painted.

Films

Show a film, in its entirety; and you have a "cool" medium in that the film is observed. Stop the film, have the children suggest the ending, and you have converted it into a vehicle in which the youngsters become involved. This "open end" approach can be used when reading a story, too; it offers you a chance, again, to get the children really to think about what they are seeing. They are so used to sitting in front of the television set, observing, and not participating at all, that this open-end method will startle them. Many, we've found, regard it as a welcome departure. They love it—particularly if you have a film where there are many ways in which they may end it.

Kinescopes are often available from various television studios, and can prove an excellent source of material for this activity.

If your school is fortunate enough to own video-taping equipment, you can produce your own kinescopes, and retain them for use with future classes. You'll find this to be a fabulous source of material. Your youngsters will enjoy tremendously seeing their peers perform. Debates, discussions, even lessons can be used—with that "open end" which brings the viewer into the lesson.

Every time you use this method, be sure you know exactly what the aim of the lesson is. What are you trying to teach your children? Is it to reason something out? Fine. They need this. Reasoning or thinking through is indeed preparation for life. Is it to find specific information? To introduce the children to a few of the world's masterpieces in the fields of painting and sculpture? Whatever it is you are teaching, determine it, in advance, for yourself. Your lesson will be far better because of this.

Charts, Pictures, and Posters Which Will Produce Pupil Interest, and Which Can be Made by the Pupils

The written word can stay in front of us for a long period of time, particularly if it is in the form of a poster or chart hung on the wall of your classroom. However, it must be suitably prepared. We recall one magnificent map of the world posted in a classroom covering about thirty square feet. No child ever looked at it. It was done in such great detail that it frightened the onlooker off. Oh, if you need to know where Timbuktu was, you might consult it, but only if you really needed to know. The printing was about the size of the letters in a telephone directory, and the children avoided it like the plague. We contrast this with a similar map, constructed by the children, with each country done in a different color and the major cities only printed in letters about one inch high. This was not formidable, and frightened no one away.

What is up on your walls and bulletin boards your children will read! Take advantage of this—and put up the things you'd like them to remember. In this hectic, frantic world it may seem old fashioned to have the children print such sayings as "Do unto others as you would have them do to you" but it isn't. The sayings of Ben Franklin wear well—from "A stitch in time saves nine" to "Waste not, want not." One youngster we know loves to draw Charlie Brown; his teacher had many posters with philosophical remarks by Snoopy, and sometimes even by Charlie. Having the children construct materials of this type kills many birds with one stone. Allow them, indeed encourage them, to read many such slogans before selecting the ones they wish to print. Have them do a perfect job. (Misspelling on a chart is very poor teaching.) Have them spend time illustrating the charts, with felt-tipped pens of various colors, and encourage them to go all out, to make their charts as attractive as they possibly can.

If you have a class which you wish to bolster in reading, you can have the names of the various objects in the room printed in oaktag, and pasted on the object itself. The children, seeing these labels in front of them constantly, learn to recognize them. This exhibit should be changed frequently.

Make sure here, too, that you have an aim in mind, and that this has been expressed to your children. The teacher who had the class draw the map to replace the very detailed one explained that the latter was far too hard to read, and that a simpler one was desperately needed. The boys and girls completed the new one in record time.

Your children may combine pictures with printing for very special effects. And, for the holidays, have them do similar exhibits combining words with illustration. This stresses both the printed word, and the art work. It's a happy combination.

If your children are having difficulty reading, be sure your signs contain the words on the Dolch list. The signs will help them to learn even the most difficult words—words which, incidentally, are difficult for children to learn because these words are relatively "personality-less." "Is" is typical. So is "in." By seeing them used in context, they hopefully will become a part of the child's reading vocabulary.

If you use the experience chart method for teaching reading, keep the charts hung around the room. When you use this method, you cover an area of the blackboard with newsprint, or other large wide paper, and you have the children dictate a story to you based on some of their experiences. You print it on the chart, and they learn to read it from there. Once you have finished with a particular experience chart, there is no reason to remove it from the room. Leave it in a place where the children will read it again and again. In this way it does double and triple duty.

SUMMARY

Simulations, if made as real as possible, present a different type of learning situation, one in which the youngster becomes an active participant, and accepts the problems and limitations of the activity. You will find a large number of possible simulations you can create, from a trip to the moon to a "campfire," done with an electric bonfire, in class. This technique may be used to teach a foreign language, or certain topics in science. Possibly the best way to teach freedom of speech, and other aspects of the Bill of Rights, is through simulations. The same is true of labor negotiations. We suggest that the children simulate Congressional committee meetings, and even step back into history by working on the Constitution as members of the Continental Congress in 1776. Trial by jury, too, lends itself to this technique.

The use of simulations will bring excitement into your classroom. If those outlined do not fit into your curriculum, try very hard to find some situations which do. You won't be sorry!

Audio-visual aids, too, can add life to your class. We suggest the use of filmstrips so that pupils can obtain the answers to questions from them—so that the filmstrips are viewed for a reason.

"Open-ended" films are far more thought-provoking as a rule than a film shown in its entirety. They can be used to really challenge the viewer.

Charts, pictures and posters can produce pupil interest and keep the printed word in front of the youngsters for extended periods of time. This serves to familiarize the children with words, and to give them something to read while they are unoccupied. Use charts and pictures for motivation, and for information conveying as well.

7

How to Teach
with Games and Puzzles

Why Use Games?

There are so many reasons for you to use games
in your classroom—but we'll list only a few. First of all,
they are excellent motivation. Children love them, and even
recalcitrant learners will come to class to play. Secondly,
there are games which are excellent teaching devices, and
others which are good for reinforcing learning. (If you're
"old-fashioned" you might call this drilling.) Thirdly,
games can be used to develop creativity and to produce
critical thinking. The beautiful thing about games is that the
children learn without even realizing they are learning.
There are other reasons which you can think of, aren't
there?

Have an "Open Period"

Every day select a time when your class has an "open
period." Probably it will suit you best to have it at the end
of the day—but not necessarily.

Allow the children to use their time in the way they

choose—as long as they don't waste it or disturb others. Then have areas of the room set up with a variety of materials. A science section, an art section, a carpentry area, a measurement spot, a reading area (a corner, with a piece of carpeting, is very effective), a writing area, and a game area should be established. Incidentally, assign one or two children to keep each area tidy and stocked with supplies. Choose children who enjoy doing this type of work.

Encourage the youngsters to experiment during their free time, with the various activities available to them.

In the game area, include chess, checkers, word games, skill games (Monopoly requires reading, thought, decision-making). Do not include pure games of chance since these teach relatively little (if anything at all).

You may want to use the "open period" as a reward or a privilege which the children can lose if they are uncooperative. Make sure they understand exactly what you expect of them, so that you won't have to withdraw the use of the open period often.

Prizes

Most people love to win prizes, adults as well as children. Notice the number who turn out to play bingo, for example. Children enjoy prizes even more—and they needn't be expensive or impressive. For example, you can use chocolate kisses or other similar, individually wrapped candies. However, other items are more interesting—foreign stamps, for instance. You can purchase a wide assortment of stamps, still pasted on their original papers; when a child has won a prize, allow him to draw one (or two, or whatever you've decided) from the lot. In this way you can encourage stamp collecting. (One class collected newspapers and aluminum cans to earn the money for albums.)

Still another method is to give chits or script made out for units. Ten units, for instance, is a modest amount. One hundred units are obviously more sought after, etc. (Playing with Monopoly money rather than real "money," we call it.) Then, when children have earned a number of chits, they select objects or privileges to redeem them. The latter, you will find, are very much sought after. Even a prize such as being allowed to draw on the board is considered worthwhile by some children.

You can take the class on a trip when every child has earned enough chits. This trip can be a pleasure trip to a park, a resort, or a fair. (Have a number of parents along to assist you.) Other trips should have educational value, but this reward one need not. (If it does, so much the better.)

If you work out a long-range prize system, have a class newspaper in which to announce the winners. Make a big celebration of the awards, and even invite parents. Give them the opportunity to feel pride in their youngsters. In this way you can get lots of mileage from your prizes.

The Three B's

The Three B's of games are as important as the three B's of music (Bach, Brahms and Beethoven). The games are bees, baseball and bingo. Let's examine each.

1. *Bees*—all basically resemble the old-fashioned spelling bee. The class is divided into teams and questions put to the alternate teams. If team A answers a question incorrectly, team B must answer it correctly to get credit for it.

Players may be excluded after making an error, or they may remain in the game and points given for correct answers.

Any material you have taught, and may wish to review, can be used in a bee, or in a baseball or bingo game. We observed one social studies class in a state of great excitement. It was an average class, but the questions they were answering were quite difficult. They had obviously prepared well for this bee. "Actually," the teacher told me, "they're having a test on this topic, and I wanted them to do well. As you can see they really studied for this!"

Spelling, of course, but also facts of any description, from any subject area, can be used in bees.

2. *Baseball*—Again, factual information is the basis. Questions have to be composed, and credit assigned to each. (You may have your more able students do this, but don't allow a child to answer a question he submitted.) Questions may be singles, doubles, triples or homeruns. The class is divided in half, teams made up, and then each person draws his question. To play this game you need many questions, so that it can be played for nine innings.

Try to encourage team spirit. Boys versus girls can often be used quite effectively.

One side goes up to "bat" and is allowed three outs, before the other side goes up. How many runs each team gets, before it strikes three outs, determines the score for the inning, and finally for the game.

Questions may have parts. For instance, "List three adjectives beginning with the letter 'b' " is a triple. "One pronoun" a single. Or "Two different combinations adding up to seven" is a double, whereas "Count by eights to 80" is a homerun.

Your questions will vary greatly with the subject area and grade level but the idea behind the game is the same for all.

3. *Bingo*—For bingo, all answers must be reduced to numbers. You may do this by assigning a particular answer to a number, and then using regular bingo cards. (In that case, 100 answers are needed.) For example, the States may be given numbers 1-50 and countries in Europe, or the rest of the world 51-100. Then, when you ask, "What country supplied the money for Columbus to sail to India?" the child looks down the list to find Spain, which is number 70. He then looks for 70. (The letters *Bingo* have no significance. It can be 70 anywhere on the card.)

Here, too, your children can help with developing the game. They'll enjoy preparing it. Vocabulary can be taught this way. As above, answers are given numbers. Then questions are asked such as, "A Venus fly trap is a _____ ." In the answer list one response could be "plant," and it would have a number next to it.

Arithmetic review and reinforcement can be fun if done in this fashion. Almost any topic can be made into a good bingo game.

Teaching Vocabulary Through Word Games

When we increase a youngster's vocabulary we increase his ability to communicate his thoughts and ideas. This is so very, very important! To use games effectively, we suggest that you first select topics and then teach words related to the topics. For example, use the topic *money*. Words you might include (of course depending on your children's level of maturity), could range from *economic, financial, accountant, currency* (for older youngsters) to *bank, change, penny, dollar, dime, nickel, quarter*. (You will be amazed at the children who need to be taught these simple words.)

As the children learn the words, have them use them in sentences.

Offer a small prize to each child who can use several of the words in daily conversation. (We love to see chocolate kisses for prizes for this type of thing.)

You may have the children play word games during their open period as well as during regular class time. Offer that small reward for each time they use one of the words you taught them.

Scrabble and Perquackey are both word games the youngsters enjoy, and they are learning as they play either game. Crossword puzzles, too, are excellent for teaching vocabulary. (Furthermore, they often are habit-forming. Many adults enjoy doing them as a leisure-time activity.) You can also duplicate puzzles for homework assignments. Your more capable children can design these for you.

Scrambled words are another game the children enjoy. You put a list of scrambled words on the board, which the children unscramble. You should give a clue. For example, the following are all flowers:

1. putil
2. laiogdal
3. yahintch
4. sero

The old word game of "Constantinople" is still fun. "How many words of 4 letters or more can you find in Constantinople?" you ask, and the children make their lists.

Still another is to make letter grills with words concealed in them. The children must find words by connecting the letters in a horizontal, vertical, or diagonal direction.

Instructions in Chess or Checkers by Students or Parents

Bobby Fisher brought chess into the public eye in a way it has never been before. Today the interest in it has heightened considerably. You'll find there are many reasons for teaching both chess and checkers. Your children are taught to think out problems, and to plan ahead. They must learn rules, and discipline.

Even if you don't know how to play either chess or checkers, you'll find there may be children in your class who play, and even if there aren't children, there are parents. Group instruction can certainly be given in either game, especially at the beginning. As with other activities mentioned in this chapter, you may be starting a child on an interest which he'll maintain for his entire life.

Incidentally, you can inject reading into the children's lives —when they've become interested in a game such as chess—by recommending books on the subject on their level, or possibly a bit more difficult. If a child is interested, this really motivates him or her to read.

In playing chess or checkers you are teaching problem-solving. If we are to believe what we are told, many of the career areas in which our children will be working are not in existence yet. However, we do know they will involve problem-solving to a great extent, and these games can help to prepare the youngsters.

Don't be embarrassed if you find the children can beat you. This is excellent for their ego and self-image development. We're not saying to let them beat you (that decision is for you to make) but that they can benefit if they do.

Encouraging participation in these games can bring recognition to some of your intellectually inclined youngsters. This itself is a good thing, because our schools have heretofore placed so much emphasis on achievement in sports, and so relatively little on intellectual proficiency, that we feel a shift or an addition is definitely in order. We can credit Bobby Fisher with this change of attitude, on the part of the public, too.

Games That Require Reasoning

Many intelligence tests have items or sections devoted to testing a youngster's ability to reason. So do many reading readiness examinations. We can take a hint from these—that this ability is important. How, therefore, can we teach it?

One way is by using games that require children to reason. These games can be as simple as matching objects, or matching opposites. You hand the child two series of pictures (even simple diagrams) and he must figure out which goes with which. You might use sketches of various animals, with words indicating the sounds they make—from a snake's hiss to the cat's meow (for little youngsters).

Matching cities with industries is on a more sophisticated level, i.e.:

Scranton	Citrus fruit
Detroit	Steel making
Seattle	Garment manufacture
Birmingham	Fishing
Detroit	Coal mining
Niagara Falls	Auto manufacture
Miami	Photography equipment
New York City	Electricity generated

This type of material is often used on tests. It can be used just as easily for games.

Another device you can use to teach reasoning and geography both is to have children "Go from Here to There." The only stipulation must be that they have to figure how people went most efficiently 150 years ago. (It's too easy today because of jets, and hence they should not be used for this game.) For example, have the children go to San Francisco from New York. They must remember there are mountains to cross—and no tunnels to go through.

Games such as Monopoly require reasoning—and teach, also, how easy it is to lose money, if one is careless (or unlucky).

Many commercial games involve reasoning. This is especially true of those produced for adults, such as Clue.

Jigsaw puzzles teach both reasoning and observation. These may be used during your "open period" very effectively.

Using Card Games

Second or third graders will enjoy playing casino (or dominoes). Both utilize addition, and help the child develop proficiency in it. They also motivate him to learn the skills he needs.

The game of "Old Maid" is good for little ones, too, because it teaches reading readiness. They must recognize similar cards, and think of ways to get them.

Older children can learn a great deal from bridge. They must plan ahead, and concentrate to know which cards have been played. Here, too, reading can come into the picture, because much has been written about bridge which might prove of interest to the youngsters. Not everyone will be interested in bridge, but, for those who are, being permitted to play in school can encourage them.

Codes

Another type of game for developing the ability to think and to reason is coding and decoding.

Children will benefit by trying to "break" codes, and by devising codes of their own.

For example, a simple code is one in which each letter stands for another letter in the alphabet. If, for instance, C stands for A in one word, then C will stand for A throughout the section to be decoded. To start off, give the children a phrase translated into code. This gives them some, but not all, of the letters.

For instance, in the code which follows UNITED STATES OF AMERICA is FMRGVW HGZGVH LU ZNVIRXZ. Then ask the children to figure out which states or cities are listed below:

1. HOLIRWZ (As they work, if they realize this is Florida, they add the fact that L = O.)
2. XZORVLIMRZ
3. ZOZHPZ (From this they learn P = K.)
4. PVMGFXPB (From this they learn B = Y.)

To decode, have the children write the alphabet down one side of a sheet of paper, one letter per line, and the fact known about the letter next to it. From United States of America, we get:

A = Z		N = M
B		O = L
C = X		P
D = W		Q
E = V		R = I
F = U		S = H
G		T = G
H		U = F
I = R		V
J		W
K		X
L		Y
M = N		Z

Then as facts are learned, they are added to the list. That is,

L = O
P = K
B = Y

until they see a pattern or have enough facts to proceed.

This type of work is excellent—until a child gets frustrated. Once this happens, he or she should move on to something else. When decoding ceases to be fun, change it immediately. However, we're sure you will find it an excellent challenge for certain children.

Commercial Games

Games which are commercially available may be just what you need to get your children working. These are games which are specifically for teaching, and are available for a variety of subjects.

For example, a firm called Wff 'n Proof (1111-NM Maple Avenue, Turtle Creek, Pa. 15145) specializes in games. Some examples of the games they offer are:

On-Sets (the game of set theory)—This 30 game package can instruct students in kindergarten through high school in basics of set theory. It encourages the players to enjoy mathematics while learning concepts of union, intersection, logical differences, complement, identify, inclusion, null and universal sets. It sells for $5.

The Propaganda Game (by Lorne Greene, of TV's "Bonanza" fame)—Students learn the techniques used by professionals to influence public opinion by learning to recognize "bandwagon" appeals, faulty analogy, out of context quotes, rationalization, technical jargon, and emotional appeals. This game is particularly good for teaching problems of democracy and debate. It sells for $6.

Wff 'n Proof: The Game of Modern Logic—This is the original game of symbolic logic. This is a twenty-one game kit that starts with speed games that are fun for six-year-olds and ends with strategy games that challenge intelligent adults. This kit provides entertainment and practice in abstract thinking.

Equations—A kit with five games for use in 6th, 7th and 8th grade math classes.

Queries 'n Theories—A simulation game that teaches the scientific method of inquiry.

These are just a sampling of the type of game put out by Wff 'n Proof.

S.R.A. (Science Research Associates) has games involving phonics for grades 1-3. There are 44 games in the program. They also offer American history games for grades 7 and 8, which include a colony game, a frontier game, a reconstruction game and many others.

For arithmetic in grades 4-8, SRA has Cross-Number Puzzle Boxes which can be used to work on whole numbers, fractions, decimals and percent, using a crossword puzzle format.

J. Weston Walch, Portland, Me. 04104, publishes a game kit called Geography Bingo, suitable for grades 7 through 12, covering (1) the United States, (2) Nations of the World, (3) universal geographical terms. Each game (there are three in the set) comes with directions, fact slips and cards for 36 students. Suggestions for varying the games for slow and advanced students are included.

Flash Card Games

Many, many uses can be found for flash cards. You can make them, they can be made by the youngsters, or they can be purchased from any one of many manufacturers.

At the beginning of this chapter we mentioned bees, and the flash cards can be used very effectively for that purpose.

Each child can work individually with them, and they should certainly be part of your reading and math activity areas. Teach your children how to play solitaire with flash cards. They mix up the deck, and then they test themselves. They must answer each question. If they answer it correctly, they discard the card. If not, it is put on the bottom of the pile. The object is to discard every card.

A similar game can be played with any number of players, except that in this game, the children take turns. Each one gets the card if he answers the question correctly. If not, it's returned to the bottom of the deck. When all the cards have been distributed, the person having the most is the winner.

Have setups available for your children to devise their own games—using a variety of equipment from measuring cups to pints, quarts and gallons, rules, and the materials to measure. Spend time having them learn to convert our present measurements to the metric system—and to see and measure objects using both. Cuisinaire rods too are useful in this area of work.

Devising Games Yourself or Having Children Devise Games of Their Own

Generally, children enjoy devising their own games, and quite often they can do amazingly well. You can too. Here are some suggestions:

1. Decide what the purpose of the game is. For example, you may want to teach phonics with it. Your children may want it simply for entertainment.

2. Model your game after some existing game. Then add your own variations. Con Edison of New York (4 Irving Place, New York, N.Y. 10003) distributes free to teachers a very interesting game called "The Save a Watt Game," which bears a resemblance to Monopoly. It's worth sending for, because it does teach interesting ways to conserve on electricity.

3. Combine games, if you like. This can add originality to your product.

4. After the game has been developed, have your children play it. Make any changes you feel are necessary. If you can think of ways to make it more exciting, do so.

5. Have the class prepare the game in a permanent form—such as by mounting it on a piece of fiberboard or heavy cardboard. Each class which follows can then enjoy playing it.

Fill-In Games

Fun games which teach vocabulary and grammar can be developed by you quickly and easily. You write a story, leaving certain words out. Then a child, or you, reads the listing of blanks aloud and asks the class to fill in words. No one sees the story except the reader. For example, you have a list which reads like this:

1._____ adjective
2._____ number
3._____ noun (place)
4._____ noun (place)
5._____ adjective
6._____ noun
7._____ verb

8._____ adjective
9._____ noun
10._____ verb
11._____ repeat of noun 9
12._____ verb
13._____ adverb
14._____ verb
15._____ verb

As the person reading gets suggestions from the children, and this may be done by asking for one from each child by rotation, you have someone write the words into the story. Encourage the children to be humorous and to think of unusual words. No one knows what the story is about until it is read aloud.

Here's the story with blanks:

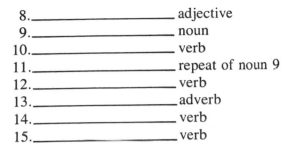

Here's one example of the story after it was filled in:

"Today cigar-smoking class 302 of Fungus Beach, Calabama, went on a trip to the moon. Their object was to see a polka-dotted train. They were shanghaied when they came upon a mysterious octopus trampolining. The octopus, when he saw the class, was crying, happily ate and crocheted."

This is the type of whimsy which appeals to children, can be used to teach the parts of speech, and, above all, is fun.

Puzzles and Riddles

Like games, children love puzzles. There are so many—and all foster thinking on the part of your children. One successful teacher used a puzzle a day to make life interesting. At Parent Teacher conferences these were the major topic of conversation.

Some puzzles have been around for a long time, but remember, even if it's old to you, it may be new to your children. For example, the old missionary and cannibal puzzle:

1. Three missionaries traveling with three cannibals come to a river. The boat will hold only two passengers. At no time can there be more cannibals on either side of the river than missionaries, or the cannibals will overpower the missionaries and eat them. See if you can find out how they managed to cross the river safely.

Answer: 1 Missionary (M) and 1 Cannibal (C) cross. Then 1M comes back. Next, 2 C cross, then 1 C comes back. 2 M cross. 1M and 1C come back. 2M cross. 1C comes back. 2C cross.

2. A man says, "Brothers and sisters I have none but that man's father is my father's son."

Answer: It must be the person speaking, because "my father's son, without brothers or sisters, must be me."

3. "What belongs to yourself, yet is used by other people more than you use it yourself?"

Answer: Your name.

It is worth encouraging the children to bring in this type of material. They have fun, but they're thinking as they do.

Commercial puzzles are available to, and can be used for the same purpose. A firm called Great Ideas, Inc. manufactures such items as Cross-Numbers, which are similar to Scrabble, but use addition, subtraction, multiplication and division.

A wealth of puzzles and other materials can be found in a book called *Table Talk*, by Martin Buxbaum. It is a collection of issues of a small magazine published by the Marriott Corp. You can obtain the book by mail. Send $2.25 to the Marriott Corporation, 5161 River Road, Washington D.C. We guarantee you'll find enough puzzles for several years of teaching.

Devising Games and Puzzles Using Electrical Circuits

One of the projects children enjoy a great deal is making games utilizing electrical circuits. These can easily be made by 6th, 7th or 8th graders and even some children in lower grades. The theory is simple. If a circuit is completed, a bulb can be made to light or a bell to ring. The source of current is a battery to which the circuit is connected.

One of the most simple games to construct is a matching type, in which, when the correct items are paired, the circuit is complete and the resultant complete circuit is indicated by the light or the bell. The wires are attached to the back of a board on which the data to be paired have been written on the front.

Since a magnetic field is created around a piece of iron when a current is flowing through it, this piece of iron becomes an electromagnet. Children can make electromagnets simply with batteries, wires, and a large iron nail. This electromagnet can be used for construction games. One attractive one was a fishing game. The electromagnet was used to attract fish, which were attached to paper clips.

Games Teaching Children to Appreciate Themselves

So many of our children need help in learning to appreciate themselves, as individuals, that we suggest you try this "game" with them. Have the children form a circle (try to do this with half of the class at a time). Then have each child tell something good about himself; something he has done, or thought, or said. As each child finishes, allow the others to clap quietly. At first this self-appreciation is very difficult for children to do, but as they start to appreciate themselves, they find it easier. Try to get them to see things they didn't recognize before. You'll find, too, that when you discuss manners with them they'll listen a little more attentively. This is because it then gives them a way to act which they can talk about when they're doing self-appreciation.

Some children get approval at home—but it is a very, very rare one who gets too much of it. More children, far more, suffer from a lack of self-appreciation. You will see this for yourself as your children struggle to find something to say, then blurt it out. Boys usually will be more reticent than girls, and will have less to discuss—but even they come around after a while.

If your group tends to become boisterous, you may decide to eliminate the applause—and certainly self-appreciation may be done without it.

Suggesting items sometimes breaks the ice—but often the youngsters use them exclusively. Such points as, "I love my little sister," or "I went to the store for my mother" are frequent with young children.

This self-appreciation, which appears so simple, can have a definite, positive effect on your youngsters. Try it and see.

Experimentation

Experimentation should be your keynote. Experiment with your curricula, with games and puzzles, with whatever you think of. It will make life far more interesting for your children and for you!

8

Understanding the Operation of
a Household, a Business,
a Factory, a Corporation,
or a Stock Exchange

All of these institutions—the home, the business, the factory, or the corporation—are vital parts of the everyday lives of most adults. Even the stock market affects a large number of human beings. Yet it is almost unbelievable how painfully little our young people know about them. It is our belief that, if we are to make education really relevant, we should cover these important areas during the years the children spend with us.

All of the activities we shall describe will have to be carried out on the children's level of understanding, of course. Some of these situations (the stock exchange, for example) are geared to the higher grades. Others, such as the operation of a store, can be done with virtually every grade except the first.

Before going into details, it's worthwhile to discuss very briefly a few of the behavioral characteristics of the children at the various grade levels.

First graders (approximately six years old) are full of energy. It's difficult for them to sit quietly at six. The more you make it possible for the six year olds to move around, and to do things, the better. They will learn far more by participating than by watching, by writing rather than observing you write on the board.

Second and third graders (about seven or eight years old) are still in need of movement. They, too, learn more by doing than seeing, by manipulating rather than reading or listening. It is for this reason that we suggest you consider the activities suggested in this chapter as an extremely important part of your program. The seven or eight year old can use books as sources of information to find out answers for questions.

Fourth graders (nine year olds) are more settled, with a longer attention span. They can really get involved in things, and love to make discoveries on their own. They will labor long and hard on projects and work in which they are interested. They often want to please you.

Fifth and sixth graders (ten and eleven year olds) vary a great deal depending on their individual development. (Ten is a lovely age.) They are capable of concentrating on problems, but also like to go from one project to another. They seem to have lots of energy, too. However, if they are complaining about being tired, it may be because they are growing.

Seventh and eighth graders are entering their teens, the age of adolescence, with its many problems. Friendships are tremendously important at this stage. Some of these young people are often torn between the ethical standards with which they grew up, and loyalty to friends. Their social development is extremely important. This can be aided by group work, and by challenging assignments. Adolescents like to try things, to experiment, to make discoveries.

It's with these characteristics in mind that we suggest the activities which follow.

Why You Should Institute This Type of Activity

We touch upon the operation of the household in some classes in home economics—but we really only touch upon it. At no point, as a general rule, do we even go near the other areas—the operation of a business, a factory, a corporation, or a stock exchange. Yet these institutions may all have a profound effect on the lives of most (at least 99 percent) of our students.

As adults, we earn and spend money, but so often inefficiently. How many people go into business without having the background for it? And how many invest money in the stock market with only a smattering of knowledge of what it is all about?

The vastness of American business is what has made possible the way in which we live—and yet this remains a mystery to many people who are avid consumers, but ignorant of the manner in which goods are produced, distributed, and sold.

We can, if we want to, include much material which relates to all of these institutions in our classes. Without any great effort we can use this information to really make our class work come alive, and capture the interest of our children. We can make them physically as well as mentally active. It will be the purpose of this chapter to show you how.

Teaching About These Institutions in Washington State's Program

The State of Washington has, since 1967, been involved in relevant career and life oriented education. Here are reports from some of the teachers involved, supplied by the Washington State Coordinating Council for Occupational Education.

In Stewart Elementary School, Puyallup, a third grade class decided to serve a dinner to 140 invited guests, charge admission, and make a profit. They all had a part—making arrangements, planning the menu, cooking the food, and, well—they did it all and cleared $16. How did they raise the money to finance the project? Answered teacher Mary Rawlings with a smile, "They went downtown and borrowed the money from the Citizen's State Bank."

There is high unemployment around the Whitman elementary school in Spokane and many of Mrs. Gerene Boberg's 5th graders see nothing unusual about being on welfare. "Why not?" is their attitude, says Mrs. Boberg who, along with the rest of the faculty, is trying to do something. Satisfaction from a day's work is perhaps the prime objective of the Whitman project which involves all the students from grades 1 through 6 in designing, producing and marketing products. "A real business," she says, "which is sort of like being away from school." Counselor Barbara Wylder explains that nearly the whole faculty was involved planning the project, involving parents, integrating it into the regular school day. A federal grant was used to finance it, something they intend to earn back in profits.

Continuity of activity from one grade level to the next is molded into a single effort which demands that all students get along with each other to achieve the common goal—sell the product.

Mrs. Boberg, a teacher for 17 years, appears excited. "Never before have I seen anything like this."

Sixth grade teacher Ed Trotter of the Maplewood Elementary School in Puyallup operates his class as a miniature of society itself. His approach, something he's been doing about 5 years, provides a free enterprise system, state and national level government, and even welfare. Students must have a source of income, says Trotter, because literally everything in the room is "owned" by someone operating a "business." Example: the pencil sharpener constitutes a "business" and a fee is charged for its use.

Trotter carries the theme throughout the day, weaving it into all regular classroom work. Students conduct "business," buying and selling services, or are "employed" by someone and receive a salary. Those who choose to go on welfare must work at state-appointed jobs, a condition students themselves voted into law. "A small crisis developed recently," recalls Trotter, "when a visitor wanted to use the stapler but had no money. After some discussion the class recommended the visitor borrow it from 'banker' Lynn Patient at 10 percent interest."

Students elect their officials (the constitution limits them to one term) who are paid out of tax collections. "You get mad at income tax time," groans Secretary of Welfare Renita Young, age 12. "It's just like it is with your parents."

Trotter feels sure his students actually do experience some of the same feelings as their parents and have a pretty good idea of the system by the end of the school year.

"When they pass a bad law," he says, "I let them experience the hardships."

Select One Area in Which to Work

Choose any one of the areas—home, business, factory, corporation or stock exchange—to work on at any one time. You may decide to devote the entire year's work to the one you choose, or to several, but stay in one at any particular time. Next, select the aspects you wish to work on. You may want to cover the entire aspect, as Ed Trotter does, or specific topics. You'll find suggestions in the sections which follow.

Educating Children in Terms of Needs and Daily Practices in the Home

Even young children can benefit from an understanding of such topics as cooperation and responsibility in the home. How can you teach these? Use physical activity to do so.

1. Set up situations and have the children act them out. For example: Mother comes in with packages, after having done the weekly marketing for the family. She asks her son to help her put them away. He doesn't want to, because his friends are waiting for him to play ball. Encourage them to really act out what would happen. (Not what they think should happen—what you want to hear.) If possible, have them get into a real argument.

Then have *the audience, the rest of the class, point out why* the boy should help his mother.

2. Do a similar scene in regard to feeding the dog, or putting toys and clothes away.

Again, discuss cooperation in terms of particular situations. What is cooperation—and how does it differ from taking orders? Why is cooperation necessary? What happens when people don't cooperate —in a class or in a family? Have the youngsters suggest and act out scenes. After each discuss it—to be sure the point of the lesson gets across.

3. Hold buzz group discussions about responsibility. (Buzz groups are groups of five or six children—put together temporarily —for the purpose of discussing a specific topic. Each group selects a secretary who jots down notes on what is discussed, and reports back later to the entire class.)

(a) What does the word "responsibility" mean?

(b) What are chores?

(c) Do you think young people should have responsibility? Why or why not?

(d) What are some responsibilities young people have?

4. The subject of privileges is one of importance to many young people. Perhaps you'd like to include parents in a panel discussion on this topic. Be sure to include the removal of privileges as a result of uncooperative or poor behavior.

5. Have a "Pleasantness Week."

(a) Plan for this in advance. Have the children draw decorations; include many smiling faces. A circle, with eyes, nose and up-turned mouth does the trick nicely. Saturate the room with them.

(b) Obtain a phonograph, and plan to use such songs as "Happy Talk" or "Put on a Happy Face." Teach these to the class in advance, or during that week.

(c) Wear brightly colored clothes. The color of your clothing does affect the children's spirits, as does the presence of sunshine—but unfortunately you can't arrange for the latter.

(d) Your attitude has a tremendous effect on the class. If you feel good, you'll find the children will respond the same way. Try to make this week really nice for youself—and it will be for the class.

(e) If you like, make the last day into a party, with simple refreshments. (Make this a surprise, a sort of reward.)

(f) If the week was successful, point out the next day that every day can be a "Pleasantness Day." Then discuss what it was that made it pleasant, and how this can be transferred to home and family.

(g) Resolve with the class to make the classroom a cheerful place:

(i)   Leave the smiling faces and decorations around the room as reminders.

(ii) You can have the children make posters saying, "Let's make every day 'Pleasantness Day.' " Or, "Every day is Pleasantness Day in Class____."

(iii) Use bright colors around the room for their psychological effect on the children. Keep your room decorated from the very first day; a barren room can be very depressing.

(iv) Encourage the children to make bright colored pictures and decorations for their rooms at home.

Earning a Living

It is always amazing to discover how many children have no idea at all of how their parents earn the money to support their families.

In the culture in which we live, most families are supported by one parent working outside the home, and one within the home. In some families where there is only one parent, he or she, usually she, assumes both roles.

If you are in a disadvantaged area, you should vary (or omit completely) the activities which are suggested below:

1. Ask the children to draw a picture of themselves and their families. Then ask them to describe their families. This will give you insight into the family situation, and also give you a very good clue as to whether or not you should go on to Activity 2.

2. Have the children interview their parents to learn:

(a) What each parent does to contribute to the family welfare.

(b) What is expected of each child in the family—in terms of work, contributions, etc.

In answering both (a) and (b), encourage the children to go into details. *Stress they are not to ask how much money anyone earns, but rather what exactly he or she does, on a day-to-day, hour-to-hour basis.* Use this as a lead into career areas, and the variety of ways in which people earn their livings.

3. Discuss or read the story of "The Little Match Girl." Point out that today, because of our laws, children in the United States are not permitted to work, but must go to school until a certain age. (This is controlled by state law—consequently there is variation.) However, there are ways in which young people can earn money. Discuss these opportunities—such as delivering newspapers, baby sitting, lawn mowing and running errands.

You may discuss:

(a) Whether it is a good idea for young people to work, and why or why not.

(b) What is meant by the expression "Self-made man." Does this happen today? Can it?

Using Money

In the course of an average man's life, he may earn from $200,000 to $400,000. While it doesn't seem so much when considered on a weekly basis, ($100 to $200 per week for 40 years), it does show the reason why people need to understand the concept of budgeting one's money. Many times teachers will discuss this while teaching arithmetic. It's our belief that this topic should have importance on its own. It should not merely be taught as an example, and skimmed over.

It's important, too, to cover such topics as getting one's money's worth, borrowing money, and credit buying. A thorough understanding of these topics will serve these children well—throughout their lives.

To teach these topics, give the children as many actual experiences as you can. For instance, ask them to have their parents telephone a company which lends money, to get the full particulars about a loan. Then have the children calculate the amount of interest they would be paying on the money they borrowed. Point out there are times when people must borrow—but that money is a commodity, and it should be "shopped for" at different banks or lending companies. The same type of activity can be done with a department store, to learn how much credit really costs. In some metropolitan areas finance companies and stores advertise their rates of interest. Use the ads as a basis for lessons.

We will discuss getting one's money's worth in the chapter on consumerism.

The Workings of a Shop

Set up a shop in your class! You can use this as motivation for many lessons, in almost every subject area.

First decide on the type of store with your class. It might be a candy and stationery store. This goes over very nicely—and can illustrate many aspects of business.

To begin with, have the children discuss the operation of a business with their parents, and with local shopkeepers. While it is very tempting to have the youngsters bring in the merchandise to sell, the resulting amount of "profit" which they earn is very misleading. This should, therefore, be avoided.

Have the youngsters decide which merchandise they want to sell in their store. Of course, you would limit it to several items, particularly at the beginning. They might choose cookies, candy bars, chewing gum, comic magazines, and pens, for example.

Next, ask the permission of the principal to sell this merchandise to every class in the school, during a specified period of time. It might be lunch hour, or at the beginning of the milk break, or before or after school. But establish the "hours" (really minutes) when the store is to be open.

Then have the children call wholesalers to determine the costs of the merchandise, and where they would get the best prices. This is important. Have them then calculate the selling prices of the items. Since the proprietor of every business must pay rent, determine how much money should be paid to the school for rental of the "store premises."

Next have the pupils set up their store. It can be at the back or side of your room. There should be shelves, and, if you possibly can, get a real cash register.

Discuss with the children the fact that the merchandise they are buying must be paid for, and then teach them about credit, and how that works. Perhaps the wholesaler will explain it to some of the youngsters, and they can then teach it to the rest of the class.

Set up the store, allowing the children to take different jobs every day. There will be a need for clerks, for salespeople, for cashiers, and for a general supervisor.

You can use this as motivation for many lessons. In arithmetic, the children can do all of the figuring—to see how much the merchandise costs, what the overhead is, and how much profit they are making. Remember to consider the cost of their labor. This is importnat, too, because, again, that factor can be omitted, and a false impression in regard to profits made on the youngsters.

Use the language arts lessons to cover oral communication (how to talk to customers), writing letters regarding merchandise, and creating advertising copy to spread throughout the school.

Use your art lessons to decorate the shop, and to make posters advertising it.

In science, discuss the value of the products you are selling in terms of the health of the students. (Don't forget dental health.) In social studies, cover the need for cooperation, the laws governing conducting a business, the jobs each of the people working must do, and the service the store offers to the community. If your store is in competition with a store in the area, discuss this, too, with the children, in terms of our system of competition, and how it works.

As you can see, this is not teaching "about" business. This is living it.

You might also consider a different type of store—more of an artificial situation, but one from which the youngsters would also benefit.

In the second type of store, you ask the children to bring in empty boxes and cans from the products their families use. The cans must be washed thoroughly and dried. If they are messy, keep them for the "clearance counter." (This gives you a very good chance to teach the danger in buying damaged cans, which might have holes in them, and into which air has been able to enter.) While you are waiting for the items to come in, have the children "make money." Have them draw simple bills, and even cut cardboard into coins. Then, when you have received a large number of items, have a store set up at the back of the room. Have some of the children act as clerks, some as cashiers, and the rest as customers. Make sure every child has a chance at each role. Have them actually use the Play Money to buy the merchandise. This gives them a chance to practice paying money, and accepting change—something which every child should know. You'll find the youngsters love this type of activity. To vary it, you can have present-day prices one week, and prices as they were ten or twenty years ago the next. These prices are available by using old newspapers or magazines.

You can teach the various careers to be found in retail stores in connection with this unit. Again, this is something the children will benefit greatly from learning.

Comparing a "Colonial Store" with a Store of Today

One of the most interesting comparisons you can make is to have your children do research into the stores of the colonial period, and then construct a colonial store. If any of the youngsters have visited Colonial Williamsburg (Virginia), they can supply some of the information necessary. This is a very graphic way to show some of the changes which have taken place in the two hundred years our country has been in existence. The creation of such a store, and actually setting it up, can be a unit which will encompass many lessons. The language of the time was considerably different from that of today. The schools were completely different, and children were not required to attend, as they are today. The products for sale will point out many other differences. The lack of electricity is perhaps the most obvious, with candles taking on major importance. The styles of dress, the food (far simpler than most of the products we use today), the house decor, all were noteworthy.

For sale, you can have the children prepare candles and three-cornered hats. Simple candies, too, are easily produced.

The prices are extremely interesting, in view of those of the modern era. Have your children find out, too, about wages being paid. Also, some of the wealthy colonists had slaves, and you can, if you wish, bring in an entire discussion on that topic.

We have found that this unit can be very, very successful. If you do decide to try it, and you establish a colonial store, use candle-light—but be very certain that no child is wearing inflammable clothing, and that every precaution is taken to avoid possible danger. This was one of the problems the colonists had—and it's no less real today.

The Workings of an Assembly Line

Working on an assembly line is another of the activities we should bring to our children through experiential learning, and through other media.

If you would like to, decide on a product that can be "manufactured" in your classroom. This must be something with a number of parts, which can be assembled by the youngsters. We have seen Christmas decorations made this way. Paintings can be done, with each child doing one color or one detail on each canvas. Games can be manufactured the same way. It is important to line the children up, and have them each do only the one step for which they are responsible.

A visit to a factory in connection with this activity is very worthwhile. One trip we took with seventh graders to an automobile assembly plant was noteworthy. We saw the parts of a car put together, and 45 minutes later an auto was driven off the line. However, the trip was a rather disquieting one, for even the children were aware of the fact that none of the workers smiled or joked among themselves, or with the visitors.

You may also wish to hunt up the film *Modern Times* to tie in with this unit. This, too, gives a vivid impression of the assembly line which the children are not likely to forget.

The Workings of a Corporation

Corporations form one of the main arteries of our system of doing business. They involve billions of dollars. Yet how many teachers can teach this topic without doing research on it? Moreover, most adults have never really studied this subject, although many own shares in corporations, which may have cost them a great deal of money.

Here is an example of one class in Zillah Elementary School in Washington, operating its own stock exchange:

Peggy Lewis, 6th grade and 12 years old, arrived at school in a bit of a rush one day recently. She had forgotten to post the previous day's stock averages on "the big board" and was anxious to catch up.

Peggy, and all the members of her class, are members ("shareholders," she says) of a corporation. "It's not make believe," she insists. "It's real with real money and we sell a real product." Teacher Dale Keats explains: "It's to help them understand the system, the economy, how business works." He, too, insists the corporation is real. He helped his class to: form the corporation . . . elect a board chairman and officers . . . issue 150 shares of stock at 10¢ a share . . . and decide what to market. "Board chairman" Dave Daniels, 11, reported that they found they had a ready supply of old comic books which they buy on bid and sell "for more than we pay." Employees are all paid a salary (bookkeeper Jean Toop, who receives 38¢ a month says that isn't enough) and the corporation pays rent to the school for business space and the use of electricity. Two students are licensed stock brokers who charge 1¢ for each transaction. Trading has been active, according to Peggy, who reported that "today's price is 17¢. That's up 7¢!"

How does a private corporation work? It is organized by people who usually become the original shareholders. They meet, and apply for incorporation from the state in which they are doing business. They choose a board of directors, which, in turn, selects the officers who will run the affairs of the corporation, and who are paid salaries. Each person who invests in the corporation receives certificates of stock. Generally for each share of stock the stockholder has one vote. Those holding the largest number of shares have, therefore, the greatest voting power, and are usually made the directors. This doesn't have to hold true of the officers, who should be chosen because of their ability to do the job.

The system of having shares of stock enables people to invest small or large amounts of money in a corporation. Since stockholders may sell their shares, if there are buyers for them, they can leave the corporation at any time, and others, who wish to, can join it.

There are certain advantages to incorporating, which you may wish to discuss with your children. For example, the corporation may owe money, but the members as individuals are not obligated to pay the debts the corporation has incurred. The debts are the obligations of the corporation, and not of the individuals who formed it.

You'll find that a speaker from a stock brokerage firm can help a great deal to make the subject understandable. If you are close enough to a metropolitan center to visit a stock exchange, that will add to your program. If not, a visit to a broker's office, to see the tickertape in action, will suffice. It is our feeling that the more we can make the subject of the corporation, the stock broker, and the stock exchange understandable to our students, the more we can possibly affect their lives favorably in the future.

Establishing a Factory

We've discussed establishing an assembly line. The line, however, is only one small part of the total picture. If you care to expand the unit into the creation of a factory, you can utilize all of the activities mentioned above. To establish a factory you will have to finance the undertaking, determine the product to be made, set up the place to do it, buy the raw materials, produce the product, market it, advertise it, and then sell it. You will then have to be concerned with distributing the profits.

If, in your classroom, you would like to experiment with this, select a product which can be utilized and sold within your school. Book covers are such a product. These can be decorated, and "worked on" on the assembly line. Another product is an ornament which can be crafted of wood or metal: perhaps a school emblem made into a pin. Whatever you decide to manufacture, if you wish to carry on the unit, it should be something which will be salable within the school. (If it doesn't sell too well, the children will get experience in that direction.) The financing may be done by the sale of shares.

A visit to a factory in connection with this is certainly to be desired, if you can arrange it.

In connection with your factory, this is an ideal time to teach the concept of automation, one of the most important ideas the children will encounter in a long time. It is truly an eye opener to visit a plant which has been automated. We visited one which was working to full capacity, and which employed a total of seven people. It is true it was a relatively small plant, but it produced a significant amount of goods. Children seeing this can be taught how important it is to prepare for a career which requires skills, so that they cannot easily be replaced by a machine.

You can tie in with this unit other related topics, such as transporting the product after it has been manufactured and sold.

SUMMARY

The operation of a household, a business, a factory, a corporation or a stock exchange can be the basis of a large unit of your year's work—to which you can link many of your other activities. Understanding each of these institutions can add greatly to the education of every child, since this is relevant and essential to his or her functioning as an adult. Furthermore the excitement generated when your class operates a store or a factory will, we are sure, give a substantial boost to your efforts, and add to the youngsters' ability and desire to actively participate in the class activities.

9

Activities
Children Need to Know
for Survival

In this chapter we are going to discuss many areas that we have labeled "Survival Topics" because knowing these things can help a child or someone in his family to survive, and where ignorance might cause problems, illness, or even possibly death. We spend five hours or more per day, at least 180 days per year, in school with our children, and yet we often ignore these very vital topics. One teacher said, when asked why she hadn't included "Safety in the Home" in her curriculum, "It didn't fit." She was an inexperienced teacher, of course; knowledgeable teachers make their curricula fit the needs of their children, and there is no child alive who doesn't need to know the topics in this chapter Teach them, please, at the appropriate level of comprehension. Certainly you wouldn't cover the material in the section "For the very young child," with seventh or eighth graders. However, no child is too old or sophisticated to be taught not to go swimming alone. Use your judgment in regard to what you want to cover, but cover as much as you possibly can.

Don't teach this material by discussion or reading! Give the children as many experiences as you can. In addition to having them write the Fire Prevention Essay (which so many schools do) have them go home and arrange for a Family Fire Drill. Make your teaching of this unit an activity program. We guarantee you that people—parents and community members—will thank you. But even if they don't, you have the satisfaction of knowing what you're teaching is really material which can save lives. Is there anything more important?

Survival Activities for the Very Young Child

Announce to your children, "I'm going to tell you a story." Go on with a tale about a child who goes on a trip with his class, and gets separated from them. "The class is lost," the little boy thinks. Then ask them "Who do you think is lost?" Bring out the fact that if the little boy could find his way home, he wasn't lost. If he couldn't, he was.

Then continue with your story. The little boy walks along the street. He walks and walks. The sun goes down, and it's getting cold. Ask the children, "What would you do?"

Discuss exactly what children should do in these circumstances—namely, look for a policeman and ask him for help.

"What would the policeman ask you?" you then question. Bring out the fact that every child in school should know his name, address and home telephone number. If his mother is employed, he should learn her telephone number at work, too.

Next act out a skit with each child, in which he or she is lost. Try to think of a different place, for each child, with slightly different circumstances.

"Mary Beth, you've gone on a trip to the circus with your family. Have you ever been to the circus?"

"Yes."

"Did you get lost?"

"No."

"Well, let's make believe you did. What do you do?"

"I'd look for a policeman."

"What would you tell him?"

"I'm lost. My name is Mary Beth Johnson, and I live at 23 Haven Street. My mother is at work. Her telephone number is 273-3861."

Do this with each and every child until you are certain that he or she knows the information, and can hold exactly this conversation.

Establish the fact that the policeman is the youngster's friend. If any child has a parent who is on the police force, invite him up to speak to the group. (We'll make this same suggestion for older boys and girls later in the chapter.) If there is no policeman-parent, invite another member of the force. You might suggest acting out the simulation with a real, live policeman.

Take the children on a trip locally—perhaps to the library, or to a shopping center. Pretend one of them is lost, and have him or her "act out, on location" what is to be done in case this happens.

What should a child be told to do if he cannot find a policeman? We suggest he go into a store, tell the person working behind the counter his problem, and ask this person to, "Please telephone my parents." If there are no stores, suggest he ring the doorbell of a house, and ask the person who opens the door to telephone his parents, but that *he remain outside* while they call.

Do not try to frighten or alarm the children, but, at the same time, try to get across to them the need to learn their names, addresses and telephone numbers, and what to do in a situation where they are separated from their families or class—or lost.

Help the children, too, to learn the location of their homes in terms of other streets close by.

Teach the children not to talk to strangers, or to go over to cars when someone calls to them. The number of child molestations grows yearly, and a great many are not even reported. It is extremely important for children to know they should not talk to anyone they don't know.

One ruse molesters use very frequently is "I want you to run an errand for me." Another is, "I'll give you some candy" or "money." Still another is, "Can you tell me where Main Street is?" You can possibly save your children from upsetting or even worse situations if you can get the concept of danger involved across to them. Hopefully their parents have already taught them this, in which case you'll reinforce it. If they haven't, you are doing the youngsters an even greater service.

Safety in the Streets

Review with the children the rules of crossing streets safely. As the number of cars on the streets increases constantly, this education is very necessary.

If you can obtain them, use filmstrips showing various types of accidents, and how they can be avoided. Some of the rules to emphasize are:

1. Cross at the corner, rather than in the middle of the block.
2. Before stepping off the curb, look in both directions, to the right and to the left, to see if cars are coming.
3. Pay attention to traffic—if you are conversing, look both ways before continuing your conversation.
4. Cross with the green light, or the "Walk" sign.
5. Never, never run into the street after a ball or other object without checking to see if a car is coming from either direction.

This, too, is material you would expect the parents to have taught the children. However, many, many times they haven't learned it. Even if they have, it surely bears repetition, and reiteration.

Children need, often, to be made aware of dangerous situations—until they fully realize how vulnerable human beings are—and how easily a human life can be snuffed out.

Safety plays, written and acted out by the children themselves, can be very effective. Encourage the youngsters to be themselves, and to say what's on their minds. The results of this type of performance will have more impact on the other children because of the realism.

Safety posters and songs serve the same purpose. Remember if something is new to the children, despite the fact that *you* are very familiar with it, it's worthwhile. Try every way you can think of to get the message across.

If you question the children, you can expect quite graphic descriptions of what horrors can befall a person—the youngsters having seen enough of such things on television.

Take your children for a walk, and as you go, review the various aspects of street safety. When you return to the classroom, have the children restate the rules they should follow. Write these rules on the board. Use specific situations, and from these have them develop generalizations.

Teach them, too, never to put anything in their mouths which their parents did not give them permission to have. This, then, covers food *you* might give them in school, but nothing they'd get from strangers. Again, you can act this scene out, with strangers (put masks on some of the children, and they become strangers) trying to foist "candy" on the children. We have heard of second graders using drugs, and introducing them to their classmates.

Bus Safety

If your youngsters travel by bus, we suggest you sit them down one day and tell them, using every bit of dramatic ability you have, about youngsters who have lost arms and legs, or who have even been killed because they put their heads out of the bus windows—and were decapitated. It is unfortunately true that if you watch your local newspaper, you'll probably see an article telling about such an incident, because this happens all the time. Perhaps not in your community, but in any number of others. Tell the children to avoid these dangers, and, above all, *not* to become a statistic themselves. If you can frighten them, perhaps you can save their lives.

Safety precautions are so important in terms of riding buses, and yet children often pay little attention. For example, if they are noisy and distract the driver, he can have an accident. Recently, a bus stalled on a railroad track—the driver did not hear the approaching train—and many lives were lost. Any person who has observed children in buses is inclined to ask, "Were they making so much noise on that bus that they made it impossible for the driver to hear the train?"

Pushing and shoving to get on the bus is another topic which needs to be discussed. Here, too, accidents can easily happen.

Why not invite the school bus driver to talk with the children—in a classroom situation—where you can ask the important questions if they don't? For example, "Why is it important to avoid distracting the driver?" "How does a bus go out of control?" "How many miles does the driver have to cover each day?" "What can the boys and girls do to be of help to the driver—and to insure their own safety?"

Another point which should be covered with your children is throwing snowballs at buses or cars. Here, too, the statistics—children losing the sight of one or both eyes because they were hit in the eye by a snowball—are too impressive. Children, particularly young ones, are impressionable. Perhaps not every single one, but many of them. It's well worth the time and effort to teach them why they shouldn't indulge in snowball throwing. Suggest they build snowpeople instead. Point out it's much more fun—because the product remains for a long time, to be admired. You might even have them build snowpeople and romp in the snow with you, to bring home the point. Photograph the results, and make a bulletin board display using them.

Both the bus manners and the snowball lessons should be done with children each year through the elementary grades.

Bicycle Safety

As children become older, they tend to use their bicycles as a means of transportation. Bicycles offer an excellent way of getting around (in Amsterdam, the Netherlands, they have replaced other forms to a great extent). However, there are survival rules for bicycles, too.

Work out the rules with your children by asking the following questions:

1. Why is night driving so much more dangerous than driving during the day? Be sure the reasons given include the following:

(a) The bicyclist can't see cars as well.

(b) Other drivers can't see bicycle riders as well.

(c) The bicyclist can't see slick spots, ruts, or holes in the road, or animals crossing the road.

(d) Unlit bicycles are a great danger.

2. Why is a light necessary on your bicycle—both in front and in back?

3. Why should you wear white clothing—a jacket at least? (Good when out walking, too.)

4. Why should cyclists obey traffic rules?

5. Why should cyclists avoid night driving, if at all possible? (Far more accidents occur at night than during the day.)

The children will probably be able to give you many more ideas for bicycle safety—as will the National Safety Council. Having the children write to them for further information gives them an opportunity to use letter writing skills.

Have the youngsters who ride bicycles wear the jackets to class which they usually wear when riding. Ask the class to decide if the color is visible enough. Darken the room, and use a flashlight to determine whether the rider would be visible. Don't, however, shine the light directly, because car headlights don't always shine right on the person.

"Save-a-Life Day"—Safety in the Home

How many people have been killed within their own homes? Teaching a unit on safety in the home can be vitally important and you can make it really exciting.

Today is "Save-a-Life Day," you announce. Then you add, "And the life you save may be your own, or your parents', or relatives'." Instruct the children to go home and search their houses for sources of potential danger. Then have them consult their parents, and involve them as well.

Use each response as the basis for a lesson. We'll list a number—but we guarantee you'll get many more from the class. Here are starters. Give these to the youngsters to tune them in. Have them search for others.

1. There should be a lock on the medicine cabinet, if there are young children in the family, or if they come to visit often (such as grandchildren). Children are frequently poisoned because the "candy" they think they are eating is not candy at all.

2. The telephone number of the family doctor should be posted near the telephone, in case he's needed in an emergency. Is it?

3. Toys should be picked up as soon as a child is finished playing with them. Tripping on toys can cause falls, and sometimes really serious injuries.

4. Basements and attics should be kept free of debris and garbage. (Introduce the idea of spontaneous combustion, very possible in the homes of many people.)

5. Read labels, and be sure to avoid inflammable merchandise. This is true of toys, clothing, and home decorations such as draperies.

6. Avoid toys which are dangerous because of sharp edges, poisonous chemicals or because parts of them are easily swallowed.

7. Have the children check for electrical hazards (they are listed later in this chapter).

The Home Fire Drill

Every school must have a fire drill periodically. We suggest you help prepare the children for a Home Fire Drill by giving them the instructions in school. (This idea was originated and used by Mr. Alexander Schanzer of Prall Intermediate School.)

Begin by having your children (if they are capable of doing this) draw a floor plan of their homes showing doors, windows and staircases. Be sure to do both floors, if their homes happen to be two-story.

Then have them mark, with red crayons, the means of exit from each room. Have them next determine what they would do if there were a fire in a specific room—exactly how they would get out.

Next have them consider the possibility of a fire in an adjoining room, or in the stairwell. Then have them, after they themselves have figured these problems out, take their work home, to be gone over by their parents, and discussed by the entire family.

This is an unpleasant subject. Very few families have ever discussed it, and yet the life-saving possibilities are tremendous. Suggest the children cover, with their parents:

1. What to do if a fire were to break out in any room of the house.
2. What to do if the entire apartment or house were filled with smoke. (More people die of smoke inhalation than in actual flames.)
3. How to get out of the house if the stairways were burning. (Jumping out of a fifth floor window is alright—*if* there's a net below.)

Discuss the children's findings with them. Take the time to listen to every child. In this way *each one will have to do this assignment*.

Suggest that the family then hold Fire Drills similar to those held in school. "To immature boys and girls," you can say to them, "this might be funny. To those of you who are mature, you can certainly see the need for this."

If you like, you can invite a speaker from the Fire Department to speak to the youngsters. You can also take your class to visit the Fire House. However, these activities are not nearly as important as the Family Fire Drill.

Do a few lessons on "False Alarms." Here a speaker can really add information to your lesson. If your community is plagued by this particular problem, spend more time on it. Go into the psychology of why kids (and it is usually kids) do this, and then cover the possible results of their behavior.

Every winter, and in the other seasons too, but not as often, you'll find newspaper stories of families burned out—and too often, lives lost. Use these examples in your lessons. *Don't, however, make a bulletin board display of them.* This can upset some of the youngsters.

Make all of your lessons positive programs. Not "We have these hazards in our house" but "We *had* these hazards in our house, and we've corrected them." (*This* makes a very fine bulletin board display. Have each child use a 6 x 8 index card, and write on it the corrections he and his family have made, from cleaning out the garage to removing frayed electrical cords.)

We are sure you will be able to derive much of value from the children, by listening carefully and taking your cues from them.

Have each child locate the fire alarm box nearest to his home. Give this as a specific assignment. Discuss, too, the use of the telephone to turn in a fire alarm.

Electricity—Friend or Foe?

"Electricity is one of our best friends." Use this topic as the basis of a lesson, and have your class list all of the ways in which electricity serves them personally. (Have each child draw up his or her own list. If you do a class list, or work on the board, you cannot possibly get everyone working the way you do with individual work, done at the seats.)

Then have the listed items written on the board. You can easily point out that the "progress" we have made is due in very, very large measure to the development of electricity.

There are, however, hazards associated with the use of electricity. Try to get your children to list some of them for you. Then teach the others. Here are several, but certainly not all.

1. Never turn on an electrical appliance while you are standing in water—in the bathtub, in a puddle, in a flooded basement. Every year many deaths are caused by this.

You can teach this quite effectively by constructing a small circuit, and showing how a person becomes part of the electrical circuit when he turns on a switch, if he is standing in water. (Some of your children can do the construction, or an industrial arts teacher can help you with it.)

2. Never put anything except a plug into a socket. Point out that

this is very important with babies—especially those in the crawling stage. Special plastic protective devices to prevent the child from putting his fingers into the electrical outlet are available for pennies. Older boys and girls sometimes experiment. In one case we saw a socket which had been stuffed with steel wool. Had anyone tried to use the socket a serious shock could have resulted.

3. Never leave an electric iron plugged in if you leave the house. It can begin a fire, if it falls over, and the cloth starts to burn.

4. Be careful not to use too high a setting on material you are ironing. This, too, can cause it to burst into flames.

5. Never put a penny in a fuse box. Use the proper size fuse. A fuse is specially made so that it will not permit too much electric current to flow through it. If there is an excessive amount, the fuse "blows." A penny, which happens to fit, will transmit far too much current.

6. Have pupils check their homes for frayed electric cords. If they find any, advise them to ask their parents to repair them, or change them. Frayed cords may allow electricity to escape, and can cause fires.

7. Check, too, for extension cords which are too long, and which can cause people to fall over them.

8. In the event of an electrical fire, don't ever try putting it out with water. Call the fire department immediately. Also, if possible, turn off the main source of current.

9. Don't allow any child to do any experiments which involve electricity without parents' permission. Even then, be extremely careful in checking for hazards.

10. If, during a storm, an electrical wire comes down (in the street) stay far away from it. Usually the storm is accompanied by rain, and the water can conduct the electricity from the wire into you. This can be exceedingly dangerous. The thing to do is call the fire department immediately.

Electricity is a wonderful servant, but extremely dangerous if misused.

Smoking, Survival, and You

1. Ask the children to bring in an empty package of cigarettes. Have each one read the Surgeon General's warning. Explain the fact

that the Surgeon General is one of the leading doctors in the country.

2. Ask the children to collect advertisements of various cigarettes. Review these in class. Point out that they never say cigarettes are *not* dangerous. Analyze what techniques are used to induce people to smoke. Some make men feel like great big he-men, such as cowboys. Others appeal to women on the basis that they once were not free to smoke as they are today. Still others paint beautiful pictures. Many are totally irrelevant. *But none say smoking is not harmful to a person's health.*

3. Have the children interview their parents and other people in regard to:

(a) How long have they been smoking?

(b) Have they tried to quit? What was the result?

(c) If they had it "to do over again," would they ever have started smoking?

Ask each child to report back to the class verbally. Have the class secretary write the results on the board, keeping a score: How many people have tried to quit and succeeded? How many have failed? How many never would have started?

4. How much does cigarette smoking cost? Consider the price of one package of cigarettes per day—which is about average. Show the youngsters how much this adds up to in the course of a year, ten years, etc. And note how the prices keep going up.

5. Invite a speaker from the American Cancer Society. Very often speakers can bring excellent films which show the conditions of the lungs of those people who are heavy smokers.

6. You may be able to obtain photographs of lungs which are diseased because of heavy smoking. It's possible to show slides of actual lung tissue which could no longer function because of the disease called emphysema, also believed to be caused by smoking.

7. People who smoke very heavily (more than a pack a day) are in great danger of becoming ill. Discuss with the children the fact that if they begin smoking when they are very young, they will probably become very heavy smokers. It is harder to quit if you have smoked a long time than if it is a more recent habit.

Deciding Against Drugs

In teaching children and young adults about drug abuse, don't ever lie to them. This is a cardinal sin—you can't afford to misinform them because they then lose confidence in everything you say. With this in mind, we suggest the following activities:

1. Invite an *ex*-addict to speak to your group. Contact an agency working with drug rehabilitation to supply the speaker. (Before you have anyone address your class on this subject, obtain the permission of your supervisor and send a notice to the parents for their permission.)

2. Cover the danger of experimentation. Have a panel of girls and boys talk about this. Have them prepare for the panel by reading articles on this subject. Here, too, credibility is extremely important. Be sure any mention of law is checked carefully. Don't allow exaggeration. For instance, it is difficult to prove any permanent harm caused by smoking marijuana, but it is against the law (or was at this writing) in almost every state.

3. Canvass the class to find out if anyone is allergic to penicillin. If you find you have a youngster who is, or if any of your children have members of their families who are, instruct them to carry identification with them stating, "I am allergic to penicillin, and under no circumstances should it ever be given to me."

Then project the idea that a person can be allergic to any drug, and that any substance eaten or injected can be extremely dangerous. When drugs are sold by pushers no one can be sure of their purity, and no one can be sure of another person's reaction to even the purest drug. Ask the children if any of them have had reactions to foods—such as hives, itching or even the "Chinese restaurant syndrome" (a throbbing in the temples). This is an allergic reaction to the monosodium glutamate ("Accent") used by many Chinese restaurants. The point of this lesson is that everyone reacts differently to different things, and we rarely know what our reactions will be. The reactions can be far stronger to drugs than to food.

4. Give the children a quiz asking questions such as the following. (Tell them this is for themselves.)

(a) Where did you first hear about drugs?

(b) If someone were to offer you a taste, or a smoke, or a shot, would you be able to refuse?

(c) Supposing this person was another "kid." Could you say no?

(d) Suppose everyone in your crowd was experimenting? Could you be the only one to refuse?

(e) Would you be able to withstand the pressure, if all your friends urged you to experiment?

Tell the children you do not intend to collect their papers, but it would be interesting to know the class's reaction. Distribute five small sheets of paper to each child. Have the boys and girls number the papers, and answer each question on a separate paper. Tell them to think carefully about each question before answering. Then collect all the papers, and have the class secretary tabulate the results. Review these with the class.

Discuss the need for strength to go "against the tide," and the fact that each person needs, really must, decide for himself or herself.

Alcohol—the Old Menace Gaining New Converts

People often do not realize the effect alcohol has on them, even in relatively small amounts. As with drugs, experimentation can lead to serious problems.

1. You might invite a speaker from Alcoholics Anonymous. Most of these people have very upsetting stories to tell. For this reason be sure the speaker is a stranger, from another community, if possible. You will find that, because the story is true, it is all the more effective.

2. Consider alcoholism, in your class discussion, as an illness which needs treatment. Realize there may be children in the class whose parents are alcoholics. Be extremely careful to handle the entire subject with delicacy and extreme tact.

3. Write to the American Safety Council for information in regard to automobile accidents caused by drunk drivers. Then assign a group of children to study the material and prepare a program to present to the class.

4. If there is a "Skid Row" in your community (and, really, what community does not have one?), you may decide to have your class visit it. Just a walk through New York's Bowery is something few children will forget.

There are a number of other situations which warrant lessons, and a brief discussion on them follows.

Safe Behavior While Swimming

1. Discuss the children's experiences with them. Bring out the point that no one should ever go swimming alone, because he or she may get a cramp, and not be able to get out of the water safely. This is true of excellent swimmers as well as less able ones, and adults as well as children.

2. Is there a place in your community where young people swim, but where there are repeated fatalities? One such place we are aware of has a rocky bottom, and often people dive in, and never come up. If you know of such a place, talk about it with your children. Local newspaper articles they read are good resources for this material.

3. Never, never swim if you have just eaten, had anything intoxicating to drink, or taken a drug. You may be affected, and not be able to function in the water.

4. Don't swim during an electrical storm, or even if there is thunder without lightning. (It may start lightning at any time.) You can be electrocuted if lightning strikes the water.

What to Do if Someone Is Choking

A surprising number of people choke on food. They usually take too large a bite (often of meat) and it sticks in their throats. Sometimes the food can be dislodged by taking the person by the feet, turning him upside down, and hitting him on the back. Choking on food happens to children because their throats are narrow. Demonstrate the cure with a large doll to show exactly how it can be done.

If this doesn't work, sticking the finger down a person's throat might help.

Stress that an ambulance should be called by another person while these measures are being taken.

Teach First Aid Through Simulations

It is well worthwhile to teach your youngsters the fundamentals of "First Aid," which include some of the items in this chapter. The most effective technique to teach this is the one the children enjoy most —namely "simulations." Talking about bandaging an arm is not nearly as valuable as actually having each child do the bandaging. The same applies to the other aspects of first aid—such as procedures to follow with drowning victims. Of course, as with everything else, this material should be covered on the children's level of comprehension.

Mouth-to-Mouth Resuscitation

In some cases of heart attack, or other illnesses, when a person ceases to breathe, if another person breathes into the victim's mouth the rescuer can start the victim breathing again. Being aware of this can enable a child to save a life. Hopefully, he will never have to, but knowing how to do this can only be a help. Again, an ambulance should be called, while the treatment is being given.

Car Safety

Lastly, let us teach a bit about car safety, since so many of us spend so much time in our cars.

1. Seat belts are a must. Children should be encouraged to make sure they fasten their belts before the driver even turns the key.

2. Doors should be locked, too, before the ignition key is turned.

3. Never run a car's motor in a garage or closed area. Discuss the danger of carbon monoxide poisoning, the fact that it is odorless and colorless, and that it can be lethal without any warning of danger.

If you have a car available, take small groups of children into it. Have drills to stress locking the belts and the doors. The novelty of getting into your car (or some other teacher's) and locking belts and seats will help them to remember to do this when they get into their parents' automobiles.

SUMMARY

In this chapter, we have stressed activities and lessons which we feel are vital for the child to live a full healthy life. These include street safety, safety in the home, fire prevention, bus safety, safe bicycle riding, and using electricity properly; and we continued with the dangers of smoking, alcohol and drug abuse. We discussed First Aid, safety while swimming, and safety in an automobile. Most of these topics seem to be very obvious, but it's shocking to discover how few are covered by many teachers. We hope you will agree that they should be in your curriculum, and that you put them there!

10

Bringing Consumer Education
to Your Children

In the course of your lifetime, if you, as a professional—a college graduate—a teacher—work for 40 years (from age 22 to 62 approximately), you probably will earn more than half a million dollars, and you probably will spend almost all of it for living expenses. (These figures are supplied by the Bureau of Labor Statistics, of the Department of Labor.) Your pupils may never earn as much, but even those who don't graduate from high school will earn over a quarter of a million.

Prices have risen constantly for over 35 years. They do vary from time to time, but they have moved steadily upward. Wages rise, too, but far more slowly. With this in mind, it becomes extremely important that we become efficient consumers, and that we share this training with our youngsters. Here, too, we ask, "What could be more relevant education?"

Consumer education can be a springboard for many regular curricular activities. It can be tied in with virtually every subject, thereby killing the proverbial two birds with one stone. But, in and of itself, it's worth covering with children of all ages.

A Sample Curriculum

Consumer education can be divided into six areas—food, clothing, housing, products and services, transportation, and leisure and education.

The following curriculum is from "Curriculum Bulletin 1968-69 Series," #14 Consumer Education, Elementary, Intermediate, Junior High Schools, published by the Bureau of Curriculum Development, Board of Education, City of New York, and is reprinted with their permission. Copies of the complete bulletin are available from the Publication Sales Office, 110 Livingston Street, Brooklyn, New York 11201. Check for $1.50 should be made payable to "Auditor, Board of Education."

Unit Area I—Food

A large part of every family income is spent on food. Children buy food both for themselves and for the family. The teacher must help them to understand that family income which is spent on food and to stock the pantry and the refrigerator cannot also be spent on other products. It would follow, then, that wise buying habits will help to stretch the food dollar and so allow the family to buy more of other products.

The following are suggested lesson topics in this area.

Budgeting

What percent of the family income should be spent on food?
Why is it important to plan meals before shopping?
What kinds of food choices must we know how to make? (prices, brands, quantities, qualities, grading)
How does planning help us avoid waste? (See sample budget on p. 158.)

a guide to budgeting for the young couple

	Lower income	Higher income (over $15,000)
	Percent	*Percent*
Total money income............................	100	100
Total for current living.....................	83	80
Food and beverages........................	19	18
Shelter (rent or interest on mortgage, upkeep, insurance, and taxes)	13	12
Fuel and utilities	4	4
Household operation......................	5	5
Furnishings and equipment.............	5	4
Clothing.....................................	8	7
Transportation	15	16
Medical care	5	5
Recreation and education...............	5	5
Personal and miscellaneous	4	4
Gifts and contributions.....................	3	3
Personal insurance	4	4
Income taxes................................	10	12
Savings (net changes in assets and liabilities).................................	0	1

(From: *A Guide to Budgeting for the Young Couple*, U.S. Dept. of Agriculture)

These estimates show that a budget based on a single set of percentages would not fit both income groups. Moreover, it would not fit all young couples in either income group because individual couples have different needs and desires.

For example, if you are a couple who enjoy entertaining at home and want space, serving equipment for a large number of friends, and a generous budget for food, then your particular plan might allow a considerable portion of your income for these budget groups and less for other items.

Shopping

What are advantages and disadvantages of shopping in different
types of stores?
What special services does each store offer?

Prices

What is a "special"?
How can purchases be timed to take advantage of "sales"?
What effect does pilfering have on prices?
Where and how can food be bought on credit?
What is the cost of credit buying?

Weights and Measures

What terms are used in describing quantity contained in pack-
ages, cans, bottles, etc.?
How can quantities and prices be compared?
What should children know about weighing and prices?
How do we compute the cost of food?

Protection

How do stores stand behind the merchandise they sell?
How do stores handle their food products? (frozen, fresh pro-
duce, dairy, etc.)
What information should be on a label?
How safe is our food?
How can children develop good relations with merchants?
What agencies help to protect the individual consumer?

Care and Storage

Why is it important to store food properly?
What should be done with leftovers?
Why is cleanliness important?
Why should labels and tags be read?

Importance of You—The Consumer

How do good manners affect children as consumers?
What are intelligent ways to respond to advertising?
What is meant by consumer resistance?
How can children make sound judgments before buying?
What do trading stamps really cost?

How can we judge a premium offer?

What factors should be considered in evaluating advertising?

Unit Area II—Clothing

Changing styles, new developments in the clothing industry, advertising and public relations campaigns, all compete for the family dollar. Children help to make decisions on the purchase of clothing. They should, therefore, learn how and where to shop, and should be made aware of the necessity to adjust wants and needs to their financial resources.

The following are suggested lesson topics in this area.

Budgeting

How much can the family afford to spend on clothing?

What is the difference between "need" and "want"?

What are the effects of new styles on the clothing budget? (fads, fashions, etc.)

Suitability

What clothes are appropriate for school, business, and leisure?

What clothes can be worn all year round?

How can your present wardrobe be adapted to meet fashion needs?

How does advertising affect our clothing purchases?

Price and Quality

How do we determine quality?

What are the names and wearing qualities of the different fabrics?

What do we mean by "comparison shopping"?

How can a catalogue be used as a shopping guide?

What must we know about sales taxes?

What do we mean by clothing "construction"?

How does the choice of fabric affect price?

How does the choice of fabric finish affect price?

What is a "bargain"?

How can we recognize a real "sale"?

What are the advantages and disadvantages of homemade clothing?

What are the advantages and disadvantages of shopping in different types of stores?

Credit

What should we know about credit plans? (lay-away plans, types, costs, etc.)

What are the advantages and disadvantages of buying on credit?

Protection

What are typical "return" and "refund" policies?

What agencies are available to help the consumer?

Care

Why should clothing be kept clean and pressed?

How can children help to keep their own clothes clean?

Why should clothing be hung up or folded carefully?

Why is it important to repair clothing promptly?

How can careful use prolong the life and attractive appearance of clothing?

Importance of You–The Consumer

Why are good shopping manners important?

What are the economic effects of shoplifting and pilfering?

How does consumer resistance affect style and price?

Unit Area III—Housing

Housing can be considered a consumer commodity just as food, clothing and other products and services are. A large part of family income goes into the monthly cost of the home. The child can be made aware of these costs and of his role in helping to make the home a pleasant place to live. The role of federal, state, and local governments plus the responsibilities of landlord, superintendent, and tenant round out the total picture in this vital area of urban living.

The following are suggested lesson topics in this area.

Budgeting

What must a family consider when choosing a place to live?
What percentage of family income is set aside for housing?

Choosing a Place to Live

What types of housing are available? (advantages and disadvantages)
How do children influence the selection of family housing?
What factors affect the selection of family housing? (neighborhood, convenience, etc.)
What is "rent control" and how does it work?

Protection

What should the family know about housing laws?
What governmental agencies help protect tenants and homeowners?
What kinds of insurance should tenants and homeowners buy?
How can an insured person make a claim?

Upkeep and Care

What are the responsibilities of children in maintaining a home?
What are the effects of vandalism, noise, defacing or dirtying property, etc.?
What are typical responsibilities of landlords, superintendents, and tenants?
Why is it important to attend to repairs promptly?
What are some good ways to locate appropriate repairmen?
How can you be sure that you have gotten what you paid for? (contract, guarantee)

Furnishing and Decorating

What should you look for when buying furniture? (style, quality price)

Where can you shop for furniture? (stores, catalogues, buying guides, secondhand shops)

Why must sales taxes be considered when buying furniture?

What is a real "sale" and what is a "bargain"?

What kinds of credit are offered for purchasing furniture?

Why is it important to understand the terms of purchase? (guarantees, warranties, contracts, etc.)

Importance of You–The Consumer

How does the behavior of children affect housing costs?

How can you help to maintain (improve) your family's living conditions?

Unit Area IV—Products and Services

Our complex society provides the urban consumer with a burgeoning supply of goods and services from which to choose. Children and adults are increasingly involved in the process of appraising and making choices. We need to instill in children a respect for the value of good consumer practices. Children should realize that money which is not wasted can be spent later to enrich living. The teacher can provide valuable assistance in highlighting the child's role as a family member in planning for the purchases of products and services. Suggested *products* to consider: drugs and cosmetics, household appliances, toys, hobby equipment, sports equipment, T.V., Hi-Fi, cameras, etc. Suggested *services* to consider: utilities, telephones, medical, legal and dental services, appliance repairs, schools, camps, public health services, etc.

The following are suggested lesson topics in this area.

Budgeting

What are some of the dangers of overspending?

What are the real differences between "needs" and "wants"?

How does advertising affect what you need and want?

How does the wise consumer react to advertising? (evaluating)

How can a family plan for making an expensive purchase?

What part of the family income is spent on products and services?

Savings

How does "saved" money earn money?

What are some of the things for which families save? (leisure, education, vacations, luxuries, etc.)

Where and how do people save money? (Christmas clubs, banks, credit unions, school banks, etc.)

What is the difference between "saving" and "investing"? (stock markets and exchanges, stocks and bonds, businesses, etc.)

What kinds of insurance do families buy? (health, life, hospital, unemployment, social security, etc.)

Why is insurance important?

Buying

What should we consider in selecting a store in which to make purchases?

What do we mean by *caveat emptor*? (Translation: Let the buyer beware.)

What agencies test products?

How can we determine product quality?

What is credit buying?

What are the costs of credit?

Where can credit and cash loans be obtained?

What government and private agencies can be contacted if help or protection is needed?

What agencies help to protect the consumer?

Of what importance are guarantees and warranties when purchasing products and services?

Importance of You–The Consumer

How can children help in making wise choices?

How can children help to care for family possessions?

How can children help their families become wise consumers?

Unit Area V—Transportation

The following are suggested lesson topics in this area.

Budgeting

How much does it cost to get me to school?

What does it cost to get (father, mother, brother, etc.) to work and home again?

How does car fare affect the cost of: a shopping trip, a vacation, a visit, etc.?

What are the advantages and disadvantages of public and private transportation?

Why is it important to know the best routes before setting out to get from one place to another?

The Family Car

What are the advantages and disadvantages of buying a new or a used car?

How can a car be financed economically?

What, besides the purchase price, are some of the costs to be considered when buying a car? (taxes, maintenance, insurance, etc.)

How can children help to prolong the life of the family car?

Importance of You–The Consumer

How does vandalism affect you and your family?

What privileges and responsibilities do you have as a rider?

What is the importance of good transportation manners?

Why should children handle money and belongings carefully?

Unit Area VI—Leisure and Education

Families tend to spend varying percentages of their income for their leisure hours. Thoughtful planning for leisure and educational activities often makes the difference between debt and savings. Children should be led to realize that they can play an effective role in planning the worthwhile use of leisure time. Money spent on education is often an investment in future earnings and savings.

The following are suggested lesson topics in this area.

Budgeting

How can we plan for Saturdays and holidays?
What kind of plans can we make for taking a vacation?
What are some free or inexpensive ways to spend leisure time?
Is television free? Is radio?
What does schooling cost? (public schools, higher education)
Who pays for your education? How?

Resources

What means of recreation are available in our neighborhood?
Where and how can we find information about recreation and education?
What programs are offered by the parks, playgrounds, libraries, city agencies, afterschool centers, museums?
How can newspapers and magazines be used to discover what is offered?

Importance of You–The Consumer

How can we spend our leisure time constructively? (hobbies, kits, etc.)
How can we help improve the recreation facilities in our neighborhood?
What are our responsibilities in preserving neighborhood facilities?
How can we plan for our future? (education, vocation)

Using this basic outline, you should work out your own lessons to meet the needs of your children.

Specialized Activities

The activities which follow are suggested for your special consideration:

A. Compare the various sizes of packages of food to determine the quantity and price of the merchandise. Assign a committee of children to buy one large (1 lb.) box of raisins, and six small boxes (of same brand). Calculate the price per ounce from each source. Why are small quantities more expensive than larger ones? Then distribute the raisins for a snack which the children will enjoy.

Note: Bring out the value of raisins as a snack. They satisfy the craving for sweets, are very nutritious and are a source of vitamins and minerals.

Have children compare the nutritional value with other snacks, such as candy, gum or photato chips. You may have the class compare popcorn with potato chips, too, in terms of price and food value.

You can inject, too, the value of natural sugar such as that found in raisins with the refined sugar in candy or gum (which causes tooth decay).

B. Have children check the sizes of products such as regular, large and giant size. This can be done in local supermarkets. In checking have them list the amount of the product (in terms of weight), and the price. Then, in class determine which is the best buy by calculating the price per ounce of each. Try doing this with toothpaste, soap powder, and a large variety of foods.

C. Compare the costs of items when they are priced in multiple units. How much actual saving is there? For example, take tomato juice at 2 cans for 37¢. How much is saved when you purchase two? Where can this food be stored? What are the advantages and disadvantages of multiple buying.

D. Compare prices on various brands of the same product which have different quantities in the packages. I.e., actually purchase two boxes of chocolate chip cookies.

1. Have children note weight of each package, and price of each.
2. Have them calculate cost per ounce of each.
3. (a) Have them evaluate the cookies using such criteria as the number of chocolate chips per cookie.
   (b) Is the size of the cookie a factor? (Not in cost. Purchase is by weight of package.)

E. Why do we sometimes purchase food or soap packages which are not full? How can we tell if we're being cheated?

Prepare for this lesson by taking a box of chocolate chip cookies, and shaking it gently so that the cookies settle to the bottom. With some products, the boxes appear to be less than full. However, according to law, we buy a product by weight. Have the children find a package at home with that explanation on the box.

F. As suggested previously, you can have the children set up a grocery store, by bringing in empty cans and boxes. Note the original prices on these, and have the children work out prices per ounce and then do multiple pricing.

G. Doing comparison shopping:

    1. Use newspapers to compare prices of the same, branded item at different stores.
        (a) Point out that this is actually the only really valid comparison, which doesn't depend on a person's judgment.
        (b) Why isn't a comparison of the price of bananas just as accurate as a comparison of a particular brand of radio?
    2. How can you compare prices which are not advertised?
    3. Why is it worthwhile to compare prices whenever you have to make a purchase?

Discuss prices of something children are involved in buying. This can be toys, records, snacks, school supplies. Have them compare prices in stores, or in advertisements.

H. What is the difference between a "sale" and a "special"?

Generally a sale involves merchandise which previously sold for more money, but is being "marked down" or sold for less while "on sale." A "special" is a product manufactured to be sold at a special lowered price.

This is a general rule, but there are exceptions. Sometimes sale merchandise is advertised as "special."

Have your pupils cut out advertisements of sales and specials and make a bulletin board display of each.

If you wish to run a sale of comic books, point out that this is a "sale" because the product is being sold. It is, however, not a sale in the sense that the merchandise is lowered in price—because the comic books are secondhand now, and almost anything secondhand is not worth as much as if it were new.

If you wish to illustrate the concept further, you can arrange for a committee of youngsters to visit a department store running a sale, and to report back to the class. Have them list the following information:

      Item of Merchandise   *Original Price*   *Sale Price*

I. You can teach the concept of saving money by buying used merchandise (by having another committee visit a secondhand store, such as the Salvation Army store) and listing some of the items and their prices; they should then go to a department store and get prices for the item when new.

Item	*Condition*	*Price in Secondhand Store*	*Price When New (approx.)*

This type of experience can be a very worthwhile one because it introduces a place to shop of which many children are unaware. For some young married couples it can solve a real problem.

Point out the following:

1. The condition of the item is a very important factor.

2. With clothing, often the style has caused the item to be discarded. If a person is not clothes conscious, he or she can often find items well worth their cost.

J. Reading and learning from labels.

Ask children to bring in copies of the instructions for laundering from any clothes they own which have such labels. Ask them to get their parents' permission to check their clothing as well. If they can, have them bring in the tags which are attached to clothing when it was purchased.

Then, review the labels. Use an overhead opaque projector to show them to the class, or pass them around. Show the children samples of the following: linen, wool, polyester, Dacron, cotton, nylon, and acetate fabrics.

Discuss the processed fabrics which are labelled "Sanforized," "Permanent Press," and "Wash and Wear." How have these processes affected the fabric? Which have advantages? Which disadvantages? Have the children interview their mothers to get this information.

K. Returning unsatisfactory merchandise.

Go over procedures for the return of merchandise which a person has bought but doesn't want to keep. Use role playing to show how this should be done. Stress how important good manners are in this situation.

Point out that the label and price tag should still be attached to the item (unless it was received as a gift).

If the store will not accept the merchandise back, and you have a good reason for returning it, check with one of the following. You can find the local address and telephone number in the Yellow Pages of your telephone directory:

Better Business Bureau

Bureau of Consumer Frauds

Customer Protection Service of the Federal Trade Commission

L. How to avoid being cheated.

The three organizations just mentioned are excellent resources if a person feels he or she is being cheated.

1. Let us say a fast-talking salesperson sells you something. You order it, and then are doubtful in regard to the firm's ability to deliver the goods. A telephone call to the Better Business Bureau will get you information. Is the firm being sued by any other consumers? If not, you can conclude it is a responsible business and worthy of your patronage.

2. Ask the children what they can do to avoid being cheated. Encourage them to do comparison shopping, visiting stores or referring to advertisements.

3. "Ask the man who owns one." This is excellent policy.

"Johnny wants a new bike. His family agrees to buy him one. He's seen a very good looking 10 speed model advertised—but he has his doubts. How can talking to someone who owns that bike help Johnny?"

4. Beware of shoddily made merchandise. Bring in a garment which has split seams and poor workmanship. Have the children examine it to see for themselves how poorly the garment was made. Point out, too, that it can be embarrassing to wear a garment which rips while you're wearing it. The shoddy workmanship can be found in all types of machine produced merchandise.

M. Buying on credit.

Since such a large amount of buying in the United States is done on credit, it is extremely important for the children to understand the different ways of buying something. Basically the family can save until it has the money to purchase an item, or buy it and "pay it out."

"Your old TV set is broken, and your family needs a new one," you tell your class. "Please bring in advertisements from the newspapers and we'll figure out which TV set to buy, and how one can afford to pay for it."

Actually allow the children to vote on the set to "buy." This should get them involved in the lesson.

Then consider the best way of paying for the set:

The family can save for it.
They can borrow money and pay it back.
They can buy on credit from the store and pay weekly or monthly payments.

Have the children discuss each possibility. Calculate the cost of paying on credit, and of borrowing the money from the bank. Point out that the family can save for the TV set, and pay cash—which is the least expensive way—but that saving takes time.

You can have the children find out what credit terms stores offer, and how much borrowing the money from a bank would cost.

Another outgrowth of this lesson: check with local finance companies to see how much it would cost to borrow the money from them. Would it cost more or less to borrow the money from a finance company than to buy the TV set on credit from the store?

Discuss other items which families often buy on credit.

The airlines sometimes advertise, "Fly now, pay later." Is this a good idea? Discuss this with the children.

N. How to decide which are "best buys."

"You're going to buy a new stereo set," you announce. "Of course, you want to get the best set you can. How can you find out about stereo sets in general, and which is best in particular?"

1. Discuss the role of a salesperson. What is his or her job?

2. Where can you get unbiased information? Distribute copies of *Consumer Reports*, the magazine published by the Consumers' Union. Have the children read about stereo sets, if possible. Why is this information of value?

3. Comparison shop. Have children check newspapers for comparative prices. A committee might check stores, as well.

     (a) Do discount stores really give discounts? Is the price less?
     (b) What benefit can a consumer get from a smaller, specialty shop?

4. Check with anyone you know who has purchased the stereo. Is he or she satisfied?

Of course, your class can do these activities for any item you select. Choose ones of interest to them, however, and preferably those written up in *Consumer Reports*.

Consider other items, too, such as the purchase of different foods.

5. Read the label carefully. Have the children bring in a variety of labels from packages of foods. For instance, have them compare orange *juice* and orange *drink*. The children will be able to see how much money is being paid for the water.

6. Compare the prices of advertised and unadvertised brands of the same item.

Have the children visit the supermarket to do this, or do it from advertisements. On so-called private (or store) labelled merchandise, savings can be very high. Have the children calculate the percentage saved. As an example, open several packages of green beans. They often are not very different in quality, although the prices can vary a great deal.

7. Be willing to switch, if an item is particularly expensive. Lettuce, for example, is often much higher priced than cabbage. Why not use the cabbage in a salad instead of the lettuce?

Have the children bring in their mothers' recipes for salads which can be made with lettuce, and for some made with cabbage.

What other foods can be used in place of more expensive items?

O. Observe the effects of vandalism and littering.

Take your class on a photographing trip—to snap pictures of vandalism and to show how it affects a neighborhood. Near almost every community examples to photograph are usually available.

After these pictures have been taken, have the children photograph areas where vandalism is not evident.

When the pictures have been developed and printed, make two bulletin board displays showing the effects of vandalism, and how it destroys an area.

Discuss what happens to property which is defaced. Do people want to live there? What happens when one or two places are allowed to run down?

If the area shows a lot of garbage, have the class try to determine why it is there. How often is garbage collected in the area? Are there many animals pulling the garbage out of its containers?

Discuss with the class what each person can do to improve the area in which he or she lives by preventing vandalism and littering.

P. What does our government do to protect the consumer?

Have a committee of children write to the Food and Drug Administration, 5600 Fishers Lane, Rockville, Md. 20852. Ask for any literature they have available. Many booklets, brochures and bulletins are being published constantly. The following is FTC Buyers' Guide No. 8 "Don't Be Gypped."

Wise Up On Shopping!

Color TV Sets Only $79!
Bargain Price
Two-Day Sale Only!

If you're planning to buy a TV set this ad might catch your eye. When you go to the store you may find the $79 sets are sold out, but the salesman has another set that "just suits your purpose." But it costs $350.

This sales tactic is known as the "bait and switch" operation that some merchants use to get customers into their stores and then switch them to more expensive items.

Deceptive sales tactics are offered in many disguises, but the purpose is always the same: to trick you into thinking you are getting more for your money than you are, and to make you believe you are getting an "amazing" bargain.

Your first line of defense in protecting yourself is to shop around before you buy that "amazing" bargain.

Your second line of defense is to protest when you have been gypped or evaded a gyp artist.

The first thing you should do is to protest to the seller—if you can find him! He may have been unaware of the deception, and can take steps to prevent it from happening again as well as to satisfy your complaint.

Should the seller shrug off your complain, don't stop there. Contact an organization in your community that devotes its efforts to maintaining proper conduct for business operations. The Better Business Bureau is a good example.

Be sure to take all the facts you have on the case with you such as a newspaper advertisement or mail flyer.

Another approach that may not help your case, but will aid others in evading the trap is to contact the newspaper, radio or TV station that carried the ad. Let them know what happened to you! Truth in advertising is too important to them to risk getting a reputation for carrying phony ads.

Also contact your local or state government agency that handles consumer problems. Many of the states now have consumer protection laws they enforce. Cities are also adopting ordinances to protect consumers. New York City is a good example.

On the national level, the FTC is doing everything it can to protect consumers. Congress gave it broad powers to halt "unfair methods of competition in commerce, and unfair or deceptive acts or practices in commerce."

To aid in the protection of consumers the FTC has helped form Consumer Protection Committees in the major metropolitan areas to wage broad and well-coordinated attacks on business fraud and deception.

Each committee is composed of representatives from federal, state, and local agencies responsible for regulating business and protecting consumers.

These committees screen consumer complaints and refer each matter to the agency best equipped to handle it, which gives consumers a fast one-stop complaint service.

The first committee was formed in Chicago, and others have been organized in Boston, Detroit, Los Angeles, New Orleans, Philadelphia, and San Francisco.

Should you wish to contact the FTC with regard to a deceptive sales practice, do so in writing. Give all the facts you have on your case. The FTC will then take your letter and see if a law has been violated. If it has, your letter will be placed in a confidential file, and the FTC will proceed in its own name.

Your identity will be protected, and you will be kept advised of action taken.

The FTC has authority to act under certain conditions:

1. *If the sales practice violates one of the laws the FTC is responsible for enforcing.*
2. *If the sales practice is of significant public interest.*

However, the FTC cannot handle the entire job of protecting the public from being cheated. Congress did not intend to set up a huge gestapo to police every sale and salesman in the country. And the cost would be prohibitive.

Keep in mind the FTC does not get involved in a private controversy. In this case consult with your local or state government agency, or a private attorney.

Keep these suggestions in mind when shopping or when you think you have been deceived:

1. Shop around before you buy that "amazing" bargain.
2. Bring your complaint to the attention of the seller.
3. Report false advertising to the media carrying it.
4. Report the deception to the organization concerned with better business standards.
5. Report the deception to your city, county, or state government agency.
6. If you feel the problem falls under the jurisdiction of the FTC contact the Washington office or one of the field offices.

FTC Regional Offices and Field Stations

The field offices are located in the following cities:

Atlanta, Ga.; Boston, Mass.; Buffalo, N.Y.; Charlotte, N.C.; Chicago, Ill.; Cleveland, Ohio; Dallas, Texas; Denver, Colo.; Detroit, Mich.; Honolulu, Hawaii; Kansas City, Mo.; Los Angeles, California; Miami, Fla.; New Orleans, La.; New York, N.Y.; Oak Ridge, Tenn.; Phoenix, Ariz.; Portland, Ore.; St. Louis, Mo.; San Antonio, Texas; San Diego, Calif.; San Francisco, Calif.; Seattle, Wash.; Washington, D.C. area field offices; Upper Darby, Penn.

Look under "Federal Trade Commission" in the telephone directories of these cities for the addresses and telephone numbers of the field offices.

Q. What is Ralph Nader's work—and that of other consumer organizations?

Have the class write to Ralph Nader's organization for information about its work. Discuss it in class.

Keep a current bulletin board display of articles from newspapers and magazines.

Keep copies of *Consumers' Union Reports* and *Yearbook* available for pupils to use.

Have the class send for and post copies of materials received from the Federal Trade Commission after class discussion of them.

SUMMARY

In this chapter you have a curriculum guide which suggests lessons in six areas of consumer education. These are food, clothing, housing, products and services, transportation, and leisure and education. This is followed by a series of specific activities: comparing sizes of packages of food to determine the quantity and price of the merchandise, the actual costs of items when they are sold in multiple units, the concept of a "full" package, comparison shopping, "sales" and "specials," secondhand merchandise, reading and learning from labels, returning unsatisfactory merchandise, how to avoid being cheated, buying on credit, deciding which are best buys, observing the effects of vandalism and littering, and learning what our government does to protect the consumer.

These activities can be used in connection with every subject area; they should interest the children, and give them knowledge which will be of value to them throughout their lives. Once you get into consumer education, we're sure you will find it a fascinating subject area—and one for which you and the children will think of many excellent activities.

11

Activities

to Teach Ecology

For the first time in our history we, as a nation, are becoming aware of the manner in which we are squandering, and have squandered, our natural resources. We are learning the unpleasant fact that our supplies of fuels are far from inexhaustible, and that, if we are not careful, they may, indeed, be completely used up—perhaps not in our lifetime, but in that of our children. The environment has taken on an importance never assigned to it before, as we realize it can become hostile if we continue to poison the air, as we have started to do, if we continue to pollute the oceans, or if we insist upon despoiling the land. The time has come for all of us to consider ourselves as agents to "Save the Earth," and to protect all of the inhabitants thereof. If, as educators, we add the teaching of ecology, the study of the environment, to our curriculum, we can reach millions of youngsters. If we begin while they are in the early grades, we can have our greatest effect upon them. "Ecology" has been part of high school science courses for a number of years, but it is not enough. Let us try to open the eyes of our children to the world around them, and to the fact that this world needs them—needs every one of us—if it is to support the life it will be called upon to support in the not-too-distant future.

We suggest you adopt a relatively simple curriculum such as the one which follows. It involves, as you can see, geography, history, and science, and can be associated with those subject areas in your lesson planning. Of course reading is necessary, as is reporting, so you have your language arts skills brought in. Art work is a logical part, as the children can draw posters, make bulletin boards and illustrations.

Ecology Curriculum

The curriculum which follows can serve as a guide and a background for you, from which you can select the topics you feel your children will benefit from learning.

    I. What proof have we that the Earth (spelled with a capital *E* because it is the name of the planet on which we live) is changing?

      A. Natural changes:

        1. Volcanoes—Mexico, Hawaii, South America.

        2. Earthquakes—

          a. California—San Andreas Fault.

          b. Pacific ring—land on all sides of the Pacific Ocean, constantly affected by changes in the surface of the Earth.

        3. Erosion:

          a. Canyons such as the Grand Canyon of the Colorado River.

          b. Gulleys and changes in topsoil.

        4. Changes due to wind:

          a. Dust bowls—such as those in the state of Oklahoma during the 1930s.

        5. Changes due to glacial activity:

          a. Mountain lakes.

          b. Land masses caused by glacial deposits.

B. Man-made changes:

  1. Pollution:

    a. Of air—due to the addition of chemical gases and particles of soil.

    b. Of land—by litter, garbage, car graveyards.

    c. Oceans and rivers—by the dumping of industrial wastes, and by heating the rivers.

  2. Mining—destroying the land through strip mining.

  3. Reclaimed land:

    a. Netherlands.

    b. Florida—from swamps.

    c. New York City—land from fill excavated to build World Trade Centers.

C. Which changes can man influence? Which can he merely observe?

II. Why is the use of our sources of energy of great concern to every one of us?

A. All fossil fuel originally comes from the sun. This includes coal, gas and oil. These are formed deep within the earth from plant and animal life which lived thousands of years ago. Why does it appear that this may eventually run out?

B. What other sources of energy are there?

  1. Electricity—which is generated by turbines which must be run by another source of energy.

    a. Electricity is usually generated by the burning of coal, or gasoline.

    b. Electricity may be made by turbines run by water power (hydroelectric power plants such as those near Niagara Falls, New York, or part of the Tennessee Valley Authority).

    c. Electricity may be made by turbines run by atomic energy. (Atomic powered electric plants at Indian Point, New York, and San Onofre, California.)

      d. Other possible sources of energy to run turbines:

        (i) Wind power—similar to the windmills of previous centuries.

        (ii) Solar energy—the sun's rays may be used to heat water, and turn it to steam. This steam can be used to turn the turbines, and thereby generate electricity.

        (iii) Burn garbage. Use the heat generated to change water to steam, and turn the turbines.

    C. Why should solar energy be developed as a source of energy?

    D. What other possibilities for sources of energy are there?

III. Why are all living things important to man?

    A. Man's food supply depends on plants and animals.

      1. The food cycle for all animals involves plants, and often other, smaller animals.

      2. Plants are the direct result of the activity of the sun.

      3. Even fish, ultimately, depend on plants for life.

      4. Animals depend on other animals, in what is called a food chain. Each animal plays an important part in the cycle of living things.

      5. All life, plant and animal, is involved in a chain of dependency. We must, therefore, be aware of the dangers of wiping out certain species (such as the American bison, for example).

    B. Our places of shelter are the result of our utilization of plants and the minerals and materials of the earth.

      1. Trees, supplying lumber, are very important in all building—homes, stores, office buildings.

      2. Bricks and concrete are made from elements found in the soil.

      3. Steel and iron are removed from the crust of the earth by mining. There is a finite amount of each mineral in the earth.

4. The earth's surface is very rich in silicon and aluminum, which are used by man constantly. Silicon is used to make glass, whereas aluminum is used singly, or combined with other metals.

C. Our clothing is now made from either natural fibers, man-made fibers (synthetics), or a combination of both, or animal products.

1. Natural fibers include linen, cotton, silk.

2. Man-made fibers include rayon, nylon, dacron, acetate.

3. Combinations include dacron and cotton, cotton and rayon.

4. Animal products include things such as leather and furs, wool and alpaca.

IV. What are some of the most important problems we are faced with in the world of today?

A. How can all of the inhabitants of the Earth be fed properly if the population increases at the rate at which it is projected to increase? (If the present world rate continues, the population of the world will *double* in one generation.)

B. Where will we be able to obtain the fuels we will need?

C. How can all species of living things be protected?

D. How can we eliminate the tremendous waste of materials of which we have been guilty?

E. How can we prevent the air we breathe from becoming poisoned?

F. How can we improve our immediate environment?

These are some, but of course not all, of the major problems which confront us. How can we attempt to solve them?

Suggested Ecology Activities

The activities which follow can help your children to develop an understanding of the problems which confront the inhabitants of the

Earth—and some possible ways to solve them. While the solutions seem simple, it may be pointed out that only if everyone works on the same problems, can they be solved—if not completely, at least partially.

Defining Ecology

To define the subject of ecology, we suggest you use the bulletin issued by the Johnny Horizon News Bureau. Johnny Horizon '76 is the nationwide environmental action and awareness campaign sponsored by the United States Department of the Interior, United States Army Corps of Engineers, Tennessee Valley Authority, General Services Administration, Civil Service Commission, and the United States Postal Service. For further information, you can contact any sponsoring agency or write to The Johnny Horizon News Bureau, 1825 K Street, N.W., Washington, D.C. 20006.

What Is Ecology? In defining "ecology," Gordon Harrison of the Ford Foundation recounted a sequence of events in Borneo that began when pest control officers sprayed DDT on certain areas to control mosquitoes and the malaria they spread. Shortly after, the roofs of native houses began to fall because thatches were eaten by caterpillars, who because of their particular eating habits had not absorbed much DDT and thus were not harmed. But predatory wasps that had been keeping the caterpillar population under control had been mostly killed by the DDT—so caterpillars reproduced explosively.

Exterminators then brought the spraying indoors to control houseflies. Up to that time, control of flies was the job of the gecko, a little lizard, but these animals, eating flies doused with DDT, began to die of poisoning. Then the poisoned geckos were eaten by cats, and they began to die—in such numbers that rats began to invade the houses.

The rats were potential plague carriers so the ugly head of disease rose again. Health officials finally resorted to parachuting other cats into the area to restore part of the balance of populations.

The story illustrates the primary concern of the "young" science of ecology: the study of how organisms are dependent on other living members in a community and how all depend on the environment to survive. The immediate moral is that exterminators had ignored basic ecological principles; the long-range moral is the far-reaching effects on all life of human attempts to alter the environment—effects that vary between *good* and *bad*.

Instituting an Ecology Club in Your Class

You may give it a title such as Johnny Horizon '76 Ecology Club, and send for information from the Washington, D.C. office.

Set up a bulletin board, with the bulletins they publish, plus any news related to ecology which the youngsters find in newspapers and magazines. You might offer points for every piece of work contributed by each member, and arrange for a trip to a park or beach as a reward. (This trip can be combined with a research project, such as determining the need for a public cleanup campaign.)

There is a great deal of information published on related topics, as you will soon see, if you personally watch the papers and magazines. This is a topic of prime importance, and should be given status in your classroom, too.

How to Work Out Problems the Children Can Solve

Have your children do a survey of the immediate area of the school, and (if you feel it appropriate) of their homes. The following questions are possibilities:

1. Is there litter visible—and, if so, what type of litter is it? (Papers, candy wrappers, beer bottles, soda containers, dog droppings, branches and leaves?)
2. Has the garbage been collected, or is it on the streets?
3. Are there litter baskets available for public use?
4. Are there animals running loose?
5. Is a neighborhood cleanup campaign necessary?

If the answers to this survey indicate a cleanup campaign would be a good idea, you may wish to begin with the "Block Cleanup" suggested by Johnny Horizon.

You may wish to take the children on a walking tour of the area to do this survey. If you do, you can point out the various detriments to the area as you come across them. We sent one class out on such an expedition, and were presented with a "gift" when they returned. One of the girls handed me a cardboard poster, which had been folded in half. I assumed she wanted me to see the poster, until she said, "Be careful as you open this." When I did, the reason for care was evident. It contained a dead rat. (The teacher should certainly have known better than to allow a child to pick up and carry a rat, because rats often carry a variety of viruses.) But the class was very proud of this finding, and, truthfully, we had never realized there were rats in the area of the school until this one was discovered. Many of the children had never seen a rat—and were surprised at the length of the tail. However, picking it up and carrying it was certainly the wrong thing to permit the children to do.

You may suggest to the children that they would like to take photographs as they do their survey. If the class discussed above had been doing this, there would have been no need to bring the rat back to the school. A photograph would have sufficed.

Cleaning Up Neighborhood Eyesores

A block cleanup may be the first step in a total community cleanup. It is certainly a project of manageable proportions in an urban area, and it can serve as an inspiration for others in your city.

The steps are essentially the same as those for a major community cleanup. Advance planning and organization are just as important —leave nothing to chance.

1. Have the children visit with neighbors and secure their endorsement and support for a cleanup. From those who are particularly interested, choose a leader (unless you want to do it yourself); or have a class member or parent to it.

2. Decide on date and time. Weekends are preferable, of course.

3. Have the children publicize the date by giving handbills to each of the residents on the block. Ask for their response so you'll know how much time they can donate or what else they can do to make the event a success.

4. You will need some money for trash bags, or maybe the Sanitation Department will donate them. (The school fund might supply it.)

5. Secure the assistance of the Sanitation Department to haul away material. You might also borrow some large brooms from them.

6. Secure police approval and participation to block off the street.

7. Be sure to let your local newspaper know. Ask them to carry the story.

8. It might be fun to end up with a little party. You'll need some refreshments, etc., and another committee.

9. Have the children take photographs and use these as part of the bulletin board display. Label them "This is what *we* are doing to fight pollution of the land!"

10. The Johnny Horizon organization will send Certificates of Appreciation, if you send the details of your project to the National Coordinator, Johnny Horizon '76, Washington, D. C. 20240.

How to Study Air Pollution: What Pollutes the Air?

You may have your children do a simple experiment which illustrates very graphically some of the actual pollutants of the air. Have each child take a piece of oaktag (called a Particle paper) and coat it with vaseline. (A very thin coating is fine.) Then have that oaktag placed outside in the air for a period of twelve hours. (If it rains, the experiment will have to be done over.) Then examine the paper. What kind of particles are on it?

Have them observe automobiles, particularly when the engine is started up. What can they observe coming from the exhaust pipe? If you happen to have a snowfall, have the children watch the color of the snow change, as it remains on the ground, particularly near cars. Where does the dirt come from?

If you have microscopes available, you may have slides placed out-of-doors, again with a very small amount of vaseline on them; the actual particles which fall on them may be studied under the microscope.

Have the children do an Air Watch of the neighborhood. Is there any building or factory which sends smoke or yellow gases into the air? If there is, you may wish to notify the Health Department in your area. (The yellow gases are sulfur compounds, which are hazardous to health and property.) Smoke or soot is usually black in color, and contains particles of carbon—similar to the ones your children will probably see on their "particle papers."

Use some of this material on your bulletin board display. If you do, this can be labelled "This is what we are doing about Air Pollution," and include a discussion of the findings, and the report you submitted to the authorities about them.

How to "Do Something" About Mosquitoes in Your Area

The Johnny Horizon campaign suggests the use of one species of swallow, called "purple martins," to help control mosquitoes. Here is information to enable you to get purple martins to settle in your neighborhood:

Did you know that an adult purple martin is capable of eating its own weight in flying insects—or more than 2,000 mosquitoes a day?

Did you also know that purple martins are almost solely dependent on man-made housing? And that a properly constructed and cared for house will attract the same family year after year?

For bird lovers and people concerned about environmental quality this could add up to fewer mosquitoes and less insect control, plus hours of enjoyable birdwatching.

Purple martins, the largest members of the swallow family, are probably the first birds in North America to live in homes provided by man. Indians attracted them by hanging hollow gourds from the tops of poles above their teepees.

As their natural nesting places—hollow trees, old woodpecker holes, and caves—have been destroyed or taken over by house sparrows or starlings, martins have come to rely more and more on man-made housing. And birdhouse builders have developed something of a standard plan for martin houses over the years. These houses are of a more complex construction than the usual birdhouse and look rather like apartment houses. This is because purple martins are sociable birds and will happily share their homes with other martins until overcrowding requires some occupants to move on.

A martin house will usually have from 8 to 24 rooms. Each of these rooms is exactly 6 x 6 x 6 inches with proper drainage and a 2½-inch entrance hole placed fairly near the floor—martins like to keep an eye on their world while nesting. Houses are almost always painted white to keep the temperature at as cool a level as possible during the hot summer months and are well ventilated with airspace attics. They have 3-inch porches with guardrails to protect the young from falling and are placed in open areas on 8 to 15 foot poles.

If a construction job of this complexity sounds too time-consuming for you, there are now a number of commercial purple martin houses for sale in garden shops and department stores.

Martin houses should be up and ready for occupancy around April when the birds return from a winter in South America. It is often difficult to get a colony started, but don't give up if a family doesn't come live in your house the first or even the second year. It is quite possible that the older males who are sent out each year as scouts have been taking note of your house and may decide to nest in it if their customary home is destroyed or is occupied by intruders. When martins do decide to nest in your house, you're in for hours of entertainment as well as fewer mosquitoes in your backyard. And once settled, the same family will return year after year if you keep their home in repair and free from mites and other trespassers—small price to pay for the engaging company of these useful song birds.

If possible, arrange with an industrial arts teacher to build a house for the purple martins. If not, perhaps the class might purchase one.

Waste Not, Want Not

What can each person do to cut down on waste?

We have been such a rich nation that we have wasted far more materials than we should have. Let's see what *each of us can actually do* to cut down on waste.

1. Wear warm clothing in the winter, so that your family does not have to turn that thermostat up when the weather gets cold.

2. Turn lights off when you leave a room, to avoid wasting electricity.

3. Walk, use your bicycle, or use public transportation to save gasoline (and improve your health—if you use your legs).

4. Use scrap paper—and use all paper on both sides.

5. Donate old magazines, books, newspapers and clothing to organizations such as the Salvation Army or Goodwill Industries. Other people can and will use them.

6. Recycle materials which can be recycled.

7. Buy beverages in glass bottles which can be returned and refilled.

8. Instead of disposing plant material such as garbage, put it into a compost heap.

9. Return junk mail to the sender. Don't open any letter you don't want. Mark it "Return to Sender," and mail it. (No need to put on a new stamp.)

10. Don't accept paper bags for items small enough to fit in your purse or pocket.

Have your children list as many suggestions as they can. You'll find they will think of others, and repeat those they hear or read about. You can make a bulletin board display of them.

Recycling of Newspapers and Aluminum

This activity is "on the side of the angels." Everything about it is good. It supplies wholesome places for the expenditure of the youngsters' energy, it collects valuable resources for use again, and the children can earn money for their efforts.

In doing recycling of newspapers and aluminum, you will need a place to store the newspapers and aluminum cans your children collect and bring in. The cans may be stepped on and flattened to save space. Newspapers should be tied or taped to make them easier to handle.

Often parents, particularly those who own station wagons, can be of great help in taking the materials to the purchaser. However, if large amounts are collected, trucks may be sent to pick them up.

Let the children do almost all of the work involved, if you possibly can. They will benefit from the physical activity, as well as by the financial gain.

Helping Children to Develop a Love of Living Things

1. Write to the American Forest Institute, 1619 Massachusetts Avenue, N.W., Washington, D. C. 20036, for their unit, "Learn to Love Trees." (See pages 189-192.) Ask for the Starter Kit. This unit contains a full program with activities and projects to help develop student awareness of the importance of forests to our lives, and of conservation of our resources. Another unit available for older children is a mini-course called "Trees Want You."

2. Take trips. Nothing can have a greater effect than a visit to any of the following:

   (a) In connection with trees, perhaps you are near a logging site, a paper mill, or a state forest. Any of these would be very worthwhile. Even orchards or woods are worth a trip because these, too, illustrate the value of trees. (An acre of trees releases as much oxygen as breathed by 18 human beings.)

   (b) In connection with animals, bird sanctuaries, fish hatcheries, even the more ubiquitous zoos, are possibilities. Pet shops and so-called "children's zoos," where domesticated animals are available for petting and close contact, are excellent destinations.

Learn to Love Trees.

They Will Love You Back.

Our Love Story About Trees.

The ecology problems in our environment today show we must begin to teach children about forests in a new in-depth way. There is so much more to know about trees than mere leaf identification.

It's time to teach children that the forests are important and why. They are to be enjoyed. They are to be used. And when they are cut for use, they must be regrown.

Now more than ever, children must learn to love trees not only for romping, recreation, and beauty, but for the many things made from their wood, and the environmental benefits they give us. They must make sure, as trees are used for the good of mankind, new ones systematically take their place.

The Issue. Trees are our most important replaceable raw material. They are not a "one-time around" resource, like a metal or mineral.

There's a contagion in the air that to harvest a tree is to destroy a forest. In nearly every part of the country, the same forests were there when the first white men arrived, but not the same trees. In the South, for example, the third forest is being grown. The first two were cut to build homes, fences, factories, barns, to produce paper, chemicals and plastics, and to meet other needs of people.

Contrary to much popular thinking, the United States is not running out of forested land. Despite vast expanses cleared for living and growing food, we still have ¾'s of the billion acres of forest that Columbus found. Two-thirds of that is suitable and available to grow timber products. This commercial forest acreage is partially owned by the public, partially by private individuals and corporations. These owners replant nearly 2 million acres a year with seedlings or seed, though most forests have simply regenerated themselves unattended. Because we demand more all the time from forested land, we have to work harder to improve its quality, as well as quantity.

Forest science and management are comparatively new professions. Where they are applied, forests are far healthier and more bountiful than even those of 100 years ago. If forests are not managed effectively, we'll find ourselves poorer without their many benefits, or we will use our irreplaceable resources faster, often with severe environmental damage.

The Importance of Wood. On the average, each family dwelling unit requires about 13,000 board feet of lumber. Almost 32% of the wood we cut each year in the U.S. goes into these homes, including their furniture. These trees manufactured into lumber, plywood, and other wood products are vital to a decent home environment, since substitution of other materials on a mass basis is not economically feasible.

Another large part of the timber harvest goes into paper and related products: newspapers, books, writing paper, film, on which enlightenment and universal education depend. Dry and frozen food cartons, computer records, and corrugated boxes are also made from wood, often from recycled paper. Other valuable wood products include turpentine, alcohol, plastics, rayon, and many chemicals. Think of wood's impact on our world!

A Mutual Give-and-Take. Wood products are only one way trees love us back. A total concept of trees' part in our world is essential at the school level. Children need to explore and understand *all* the uses for the forests: recreation, wildlife, watershed protection, and tree growth for environment and better living. They should realize that our knowledge of forestry must be put to work for the future of all of us, and all who come after us.

Your students should know some forestry history; how careless logging once needlessly eliminated wildlife sanctuaries and seriously affected soil and water conservation. They should understand how  through public concern and their own efforts, both big industrial owners and forest owners with only two dozen acres of land have become scientific tree farmers to insure continuing bounty of the forest.

They should research increased fire, insect and disease protection, better use of timber in the woods, in manufacturing plants; trees' part in city planning; why forests need roads through them (what do you do when you have a forest fire to fight and no way to get to it?). They should know research is being done on air pollutants damage to trees, so that in the future, strains more resistant to pollution can be planned for problem areas.

Trees and Our Environment. Equally important, students need to understand the roles trees have in the natural environment. Trees purify water and air, and conserve soil. While growing, trees return pure oxygen to the air, and young trees give off more oxygen than old ones. An acre of fast-growing stock releases as much oxygen as is breathed by 18 human beings.

Trees cool the air. Young minds gain new respect for an ordinary elm tree when they learn that on a hot summer day, it will transpire 7 tons of water, and that evaporation produces the same cooling effect as 10 room air conditioners running 20 hours. (We've startled some adults with that fact, too!) Trees' cooling effect can be felt through a walk around a large city park and then out on surrounding streets.

Trees can reduce highway noise by as much as 50%, even more in cities. Solid belts of trees, with shrub-row plantings on the ground, provide a dense barrier to sound waves, especially effective along freeways and in residential areas.

From the forested third of the country comes three-fourths of the nation's water for human needs. Trees act as a "canopy" to cushion the impact of rainfall on forest floors; they regulate water flow, and are a crucial link in the earth's water system.

The forest furnishes the environmental elements of food, water, and cover for wildlife. Where trees are harvested in patches, shrubs, bushes and seedlings abound. Birds and animals find both food and cover along these edges, and multiply.

Trees for Recreation. Use of the outdoors for recreation is part of the American way of life all students love. As population, leisure time, income and mobility have increased, demands upon forested land for hunting, fishing, skiing, camping, hiking, and riding have risen dramatically. National and state forests host millions of visitors annually. The use of privately owned land by the public for recreation is also increasing. A few years ago, a survey of 66 million acres owned by forest industries showed 95% of it open for some form of recreation.

In the future, people will have more leisure, and travel more. Forested land must be managed even more effectively to maintain proper balance and accessibility, from remote wilderness to city parks, used daily by thousands.

Trees for Today and Tomorrow. America needs wood; products for American use, environment for Americans to live in, trees for Americans to play amongst. Trees grow into forests. Forests give products. Trees need to be regrown.

Today's turnover of trees becomes something to care about, very much.

And now . . . just what can you do.

Set up a Learn to Love Trees program for your class.

We suggest a month-long study with activities and projects to help develop student awareness of forest contributions and outdoor conservation. Think of the impact of even 100 schools in your state, times all the states across the nation, all taking part in a Learn To Love Trees program.

Write us about what your school does and how it worked, how the students liked it. We'll send your class a personalized Certificate of Accomplishment.

1. Write to us for our Learn to Love Trees Starter Kit. It contains a 25' x 35' full color chart — Growth of a Tree, with a pamphlet of teaching suggestions, and a similar map of

Forests and Trees of the U.S., also with a booklet of class projects. A bibliography of other materials is also in it.

2. Check local libraries and your state forestry or conservation department for films on the forest, paper and lumber production, etc.

3. Nearly every state department of forestry maintains tree nurseries where seedlings can be obtained for a few cents each. See what is best to plant this spring in your area by writing to the state forestry department.

Now you're ready to start Learn to Love Trees Month, an in-depth plan for classroom adaptation!

Week One

1. Set The Scene. Spend your initial session explaining the program. Interpret our Love Story. Scan the class for thoughts about trees. What do students like best, what's important to them about trees? Have them name fun times they remember about trees. Ask them to bring in snapshots or clippings of recreational or useful things about trees.

2. Divide into Research Groups. Divide classroom into study and research groups by category: a) how we use forests (recreation, commercial timber, environment, wildlife, etc.). b) forestry (conservation, reseeding, forest management, tree farms, how forests are grown, identification of trees, location of species, c) study of products (lumber for building, plywood, paper, charcoal, fruit, etc.)

3. Start Scrapbooks of Projects. Have each student start a scrapbook for future discussion. Start him collecting snapshots or magazine clippings and articles illustrating information on his subject.

4. Decorate Your Room. Make a bulletin board of snapshots children bring in showing "Why Love Trees." Simple shots of picnics or rough-and-tumble games beneath a tree, a snap of one boy's treehouse, another's model ship. Add photographs of forests, products, etc. Take an available wall area to develop a "Why Trees are Important" display. Use brown paper cut into trunk-and-branches, mount on wall, post informative materials on it. Get some chicken wire for a base and build a model tree. Put newspaper around the wire base and cover with brown crepe paper. Try a giant paper mache tree.

5. Display and Discuss Visual Aids. Display charts, maps, materials from your starter kit. Have supplemental ones made up by students. Show available films, play audio tapes.

6. Library Day. Name a Library Day for collection of materials on research projects assigned to students.

Week Two

1. Field Trips. Plan at least one good field trip. Maybe you're located near a logging site, a paper mill, a state forest. Tour a newspaper plant, discover an orchard, plan a picnic in an interesting woods. Find a home that's in the exposed-lumber stage of building and take with you the facts about what wood means to the home building industry. Almost every school has access to tree-lined city streets, a city park, (note coolness and noise factors as you stroll). If your city has a city planning committee, visit the office and discuss trees' part in city planning.

Don't forget to visit a lumber yard. Have someone talk to the group about supply and demand. If you're anywhere near one, plan a field trip to a Maple Sugar Festival.

2. Experiments and Science Projects. Our "Growth of a Tree" brochure in the starter set is packed with teaching suggestions and experiments for outdoor science, also classroom ideas for science and language art projects. Relate these to your field trips wherever possible.

3. Personal Visual Records. Put learning into pictures. Bring cameras along on field trips. Have students take snaps to add to their class project scrapbooks. Upon returning from field trips, have them make notes of observations. If a home movie or slide camera is available, try the fun of "home movies." Activities, displays, field trips — record them all, then put on a show.

4. Scale Models of Learning. Have students build scale models for visual study of the many aspects of the forests. Themes can be recreation forests, logging, water and rain supply in forests, wildlife conservation, visualizing how air and temperature are affected by trees. Be sure to have one exhibit on city planning, showing how trees are planted for noise reduction and shade, minipark for shoppers' cooling off and resting.

Students interested in carpentry can build a lumber framework house display to point up the impact trees have on the home building industry. (Many lumber yards have bins of scrap lumber available free of charge).

Your classroom scale models can be made from paper mache, clay or, logically, wood. They can be done on a large scale for total classroom participation, or have each student plan his own in a shoebox!

Week Three

1. Panel Discussions. Set up an official panel discussion group based on students' projects from Week One. As week progresses, let each student have the opportunity to read and discuss his scrapbook content with class. Set up debates about forest and national timber supply, forests and the environment, and so forth.

2. Tree Buddy System. Show the children how they can personally become involved. Have each one talk with at least one adult during the week to explain about forest management, tree farms, ownership of private wooded lots. Have student bring in signed note "Johnny Smith talked to me about forests today."

3. Poster Contest. Conduct an art poster competition on subject(s) pertinent to using and regrowing forests, recreation, fire

prevention, anti-litter, uses of wood, planting seedlings.

4. Plan or Plant Seedlings. Have students plan areas for new trees at school and in their community. Plantings can be set for a proper time, with official ceremonies. Have students find spots around home or in city areas that need trees. Some city streets have no trees between sidewalk and street area. If this area is controlled by your city, have class contact officials to see if trees can be planted. Invite a state or federal or industrial forester, if one is nearby, to talk about care of trees.

Week Four

1. PTA Seminar. Arrange with your school PTA to have a Learn To Love Trees program for one meeting. Use a student panel discussion or parent-teacher-student question and answer format. Show any home movies or slides you may have taken.

2. School Fair. The ideal climax to your Learn To Love Trees program is a FAIR! Open it to the rest of the school, to parents for a weekend or evening, or even to the community. Table displays of wood products can be supplemented with cards or student guides explaining, "how could we have books if we didn't begin with wood."

Have "stump the adults" (or other grades) games with prizes for leaf or tree identification or brain teasers the students make up (Which has more cooling power, an elm tree or 10 room air conditioners?)

Use your classroom displays and scale models for exhibits. Have students explain.

Set up a booth to sell products made from wood. Let students bring in "white elephants" from home; anything from pencils or back issues of magazines, to donated maple sugar candy, use their imagination! Sell "Trees" literature at cost or 5¢ profit (see order information in AIDS).

More elaborately, your fair can encompass involved science exhibits, as areas of water and rain supply, planning and growth of forests, steps from timber-to-paper. All are especially effective for display ideas.

3. Messages to The Community. Let the kids be something big in their community. Set up a news conference about what you've done during Learn To Love Tree month. Call a local newspaper for a novel bit of news. Young school kids are tackling a national concern in a new way. Try a radio or TV news contact for an impromptu interview with students about their projects, and what they can tell adults about trees today.

Then don't forget to write us about what you did and send newspaper clippings when you make the papers!

American Forest Institute

1619 Massachusetts Avenue N.W., Washington, D.C. 20036 (202) 667-7807

(c) If you teach in the city, is there a farm, an honest-to-goodness farm you might take your children to? You should take a poll of your children to determine whether or not this is a good idea. As we said before, often teachers are very much surprised by the number of city children who have never, even seen a cow.

Growing Things in the Classroom

Earlier in this book we mentioned the excitement of growing things in the classroom. In terms of ecology this is very important. Green plants can be used to teach the children how the plants manufacture food—and since it is this source which is the basic supplier of all of the food on the earth, children should be taught exactly how the process, which is called photosynthesis, works. The four requirements for the process to take place are chlorophyl (the green coloring matter in all green plants), sunshine, water, and carbon dioxide (one of the gases normally found in the air). You can find simple experiments to show the process in action.

Animals, too, such as chameleons, are fascinating, and require little care. Gold or tropical fish require more care, but are very worthwhile. The same is true of parakeets, white mice, gerbils, even canaries. Hamsters, small alligators, even guinea pigs (which are not really pigs at all, but rodents) make excellent classroom attractions. You will need to have some child take home any living thing over weekends or holidays. Care and gentle handling should be stressed. If the purpose of teaching is to develop a reverence for life, all life must be carefully nurtured.

Making a Compost Pile

A good compost pile is a big help to any gardener, no matter how big or small his garden is. The end product of a compost pile is a soil which is exceedingly rich in humus content and in plant nutrients. Such soil is very good for potting house plants and for planting seeds.

Compost is almost always made out-of-doors, in partial sun. Almost any kind of living material is good. (Only diseased plants should be avoided.) Grass clippings, sod, weeds, refuse from vegetables, and all types of animal manures can be used. All of this decomposes to form new soil. The process may be aided by the addition of an occasional sprinkling of ground limestone to the pile, and it should be kept moist. If there is not enough rain, water should be added, and the top of the pile kept concave to catch as much rainwater as possible. It takes a period of months to convert the material put on the pile into humus. It depends on the climate—warmer places require less time. There are commercial activators available which speed up the process of decomposition, to such an extent that it is possible to obtain an excellent humus in three or four months.

If you have any land available around the school building you can set up a compost heap. A miniature one can be made in the classroom, but be sure it gets sunshine and water.

Actually Plant Trees

It is a very exciting project to plant a tree with every class you teach. The children associate themselves with this tree, and watch its growth long after they leave your jurisdiction. Mimosa trees are quick-growing and because of this are excellent for your purpose, providing they will do well in your particular climate. Weeping willows are fast-growing, too, but their roots attack the sewer pipes, and you can cause expensive plumbing repairs to become necessary. Other types of trees, such as birch, are attractive, as are the flowering fruit trees.

You can, of course, plant more than one. Trees put a large amount of oxygen into the air, and so add to the quality of the air we breathe.

You may try transplanting trees, but this may or may not work out well, depending on whether or not the roots are damaged.

Put a small label on each tree, commemorating the event of its planting. It is possible for the children to earn the money necessary to buy the trees from the proceeds of their recycling activities.

Experimenting with Solar Energy

Encourage your children to rig up experiments using solar energy to heat something. It may be a container of water, in which case they can insert a thermometer in the water, and learn the exact number of degrees the temperature is raised. It might be to raise the temperature of alcohol, which will cause the liquid to evaporate. Encourage them to think up various ways to show the effects of the sun's energy, and utilize these. Keep watch, too, for articles on the subject. We believe these will be forthcoming as more and more experimentation is done in this area.

The Oceans–the Last Frontier on Earth

The oceans cover approximately five-sevenths of the Earth's surface, and contain an unbelievably large amount of protein, which could help to feed the as yet unborn billions who will inhabit the Earth. The oceans also contain minerals in staggeringly large amounts, and sources of oil which we are now tapping.

Do a unit studying the ocean. As was suggested earlier in this book, if possible, take your class on a trip to observe the ocean in action. Even if you cannot, use current events to motivate the unit. Newspapers report conditions in Hawaii, for example, when there are huge waves. Tidal waves are a special case, associated with upheavals of the ocean floor.

Bring to the attention of the children the possibility of using tidal energy as a source of power.

You can bring in SCUBA equipment, and if you, or anyone in the class (or a parent) is knowledgeable, teach some of the techniques to the youngsters.

Underwater photography is a fascinating topic. Kinescopes are available of some of Jacques Cousteau's films.

You can have the children study and make models of the floor of the ocean, showing the deep ocean floor, the rise, the continental slope, the continental shelf, and the land mass which forms shorelines.

From actual shorelines you can take samples of sand, which can be examined under the microscope.

A unit on "life in the sea" can be extremely rewarding, as your children study creatures they have never heard about, such as fish that cross land (coelacanths), electric eels, and dolphins which communicate with one another and with their trainers, when in captivity.

The age-old question has puzzled man for centuries—and will puzzle your children, too. How deep is the ocean? It varies greatly, but indeed, the ocean is still the last frontier.

Other Activities for Study of the Environment

Why not have your children do a moon watch—studying the appearance of the moon at the same time every evening for several months? Consider doing weather watches, too, and comparing the weather forecasts with weather reports. Clouds, too, form a fascinating unit for study, as do storms of all kinds. The weather maps in the daily newspaper are a source of interesting material.

The sun, the moon, the stars, all are part of the environment, and have a marked influence on our lives.

Ecology is a study which combines many, many theoretical aspects of science. But it is a practical science, too, and it is with a view toward extreme practicality that we believe you should teach it.

SUMMARY

Ecology is among the newest of our educational concerns, and will continue to be indefinitely. It deserves the attention of every teacher. In this chapter you have a simple curriculum to help you to select topics of interest for your children–and which you can gear to their levels of comprehension. The major topics include the changing Earth, the need for new sources of energy, the importance and interrelationship of all living things, and the problems we all face today and in the future.

Our government has instituted a campaign for ecological improvement, called Johnny Horizon. Samples of suggested programs are included in this chapter. It is suggested that you institute an ecology club, that you stress "Waste not, want not," that you involve your children in activities such as planting trees, recycling aluminum and newspapers, studying solar energy and the oceans, and taking up current problems such as air pollution.

Ecology is as broad as the whole Earth. Let's make it so in our classrooms as well. The improvement we make will benefit our youngsters, and their youngsters, as well.

12

More than a Score of Ideas
to Make Reading Fun

Let us face it! No matter how much we teach
our children— and about how many different subjects—our
work is usually judged by the amount of progress our children make in reading. Generally this progress is judged by
the years of growth shown by standardized reading test results. However, growth can be seen in other ways, as well.
For example, "Bobbie is reading much more these days
than he ever did before," Mrs. Evans reports. And she's
right! This, too, reflects growth.

It is our belief that if you get your students to read for
pleasure, they will show an improvement in their standardized reading test results as well. With this in mind, we have
some suggestions which you should find of value.

Visit the Local and the School Libraries

Take every child to the library in your community at
least once to introduce it, and to help him feel comfortable
there. (All trips are worthwhile, but one is essential.) En-

courage every youngster to join the library, and to get a library card.

Motivate them by putting up a huge poster in your room, with the caption "We Have Joined the Public Library." Then allow each child to sign his or her name. If the youngster is too young, put the names on yourself.

If you teach young children, and your library has a story hour, take them to it.

Make the library a pleasant place for the children, so they will want to go there. In some communities there are films shown at specific times, for the same purpose.

Also familiarize your class with the school library.

One teacher called the library "The Treasure House for Everyone." She had a tremendous poster with an empty treasure chest. Each time a youngster finished reading a book, he or she could draw a simple book, with the title, sign his or her name, and paste it on. The children loved it. By the end of the year the chest was overflowing!

Magazine and Library Corner

Set up a corner of your room with books and magazines. Check the book room. We're sure you'll find much you can use. Also, ask your children to bring in books and magazines they've read and enjoyed—if they and their parents are willing to part with them. For example, copies of *Reader's Digest, Sports Illustrated,* or *National Geographic* are excellent.

If you purchase books from commercial companies such as Scholastic's TAB (Teenage Book Club) you can earn valuable bonuses to help stock the library.

Still another source may be books borrowed from your school library.

Once you have the materials, have the youngsters draw lots for serving as class librarians. (Use two or three.) Have a time at the beginning or the end of the period for the class to browse, borrow and read the books and magazines.

The question of comic books always comes up. We see no reason why they can't be used, although we suggest eliminating the violent or lurid ones.

Also allow the children to read when they've finished the work assigned to them.

Try to find books or magazines which will interest each child. Include sports, movies, animals and people.

Choose Exciting Reading Materials

The advertisement shown on page 200 will give you some idea of the type of exciting reading materials which are available today. In this era of television and movies, with cops and robbers, cowboys and counter-espionage, how can we hand our children Tom, Dick and Jane, and expect all of them to learn? Oh, some youngsters very dutifully will. Others, too, will read almost because it comes so naturally for them. But for your child who needs to be motivated, and whose imagination must be stimulated, there are now available very special reading materials.

You will note that this advertisement mentions "high school students who haven't mastered basic skills." It is suitable, we feel, for many elementary school students—particularly those who have been held over, and who are much older than their classmates. In our six to eight grade school (intermediate), the range goes from ten through fifteen years of age.

Your choice of materials can make a big difference in the youngsters' motivation. It's worth begging, or borrowing the funds to try to obtain books, kits, or magazines which they will enjoy, and to which they can relate. Many magazines, such as those published by Scholastic, fit the bill beautifully. (For full information, write to Scholastic, Englewood Cliffs, N. J.)

A Period for Pleasure Reading

Once in a while you can use a full period for pleasure reading as a "reward" for good work. If you do this, read something yourself. Let the children see you reading. Can you imagine how seldom some of our boys and girls see anyone reading? And wouldn't that be a reward for you, too?

Form a Contributing Class Book Club

It has been suggested that a class book club be formed. Every student invests $1, with which the teacher buys paperbacks. If these

are bought from a book club, bonuses can be obtained, which will swell the number in the library.

Carefully select the books—and get books the youngsters will like. Have the books circulate constantly. At the end of the school year, have a lottery; each student should get back two books, but he will have had access during the year to 75 or more.

Use the Daily Newspapers

In connection with almost every subject area you can use newspapers. The boy who will be interested in little else may read the sports pages—or the murder trials. The human interest stories, too, are good for our purposes. Even astrology has proved to be intriguing. Encourage the children, too, to do the crossword puzzles for vocabulary building.

Riddles and Jokes

In the variety stores you can obtain joke books, and books of riddles and puzzles, particularly crossword puzzles. All are good for reading. Try having some of these read aloud, and used with an entire class.

Progress Cards

Children gain satisfaction by seeing their own progress. An easy way to show this is by the use of Progress Cards. Use 8½ x 14 cards. Divide each card into 3 or 4 columns for the child to list the different types of material he has read, i.e., books read, short stories, magazine articles and miscellaneous materials. Keep the card file in a prominent place in your room.

Using Television Scripts

One highly successful experimental reading program involves using television scripts along with kinescopes of various programs such as "I Love Lucy." The children read the scripts as they follow the program. They later act out the script, first reading the parts silently and then aloud.

Plays Are Fun to Read

We've found that your youngsters enjoy reading plays aloud. You can probably find in your school library both play anthologies and single copies of plays. If you so desire, you can make copies of scripts using duplicating equipment. There is no need to produce each play, although you may decide to do that, too.

Selecting Reading Materials

Obtain reading materials the children will be attracted to and will enjoy. For little ones, brightly colored illustrations add a great deal. Display such books around the room, and permit the children to browse and to make their own selections. You may be quite surprised by their choices.

Older children deserve a wide choice of books, too. Try to find topics of interest. Discover subjects your children are drawn to, and get books for them. Mysteries (on the youngsters' level) are usually successful. Girls of ten love stories of horses. Animals, romance, science fiction—try them all. (Read all books yourself—unless they appear on a "recommended" list.)

Reading Aloud

Read sections of books aloud—giving the flavor but not the endings. Try to whet the youngsters' appetites.

You may have children select portions of books they are reading, or have read and enjoyed, for this oral reading.

Read as dramatically as you possibly can. Remember—we have to compete with television.

Encourage Children to Build Their Own Libraries

Give books as prizes, and you may even want to hold a used book fair, where books should be sold for 25¢ or less. (What more relevant recycling is possible?)

Posters Advertising Books

Have your children make posters advertising books. Drawings, paintings, cartoons, montages, magazine illustrations are all suitable for this purpose.

Use Your School Publications

Use previous copies of your school literary magazine. Youngsters enjoy reading other children's work, and you can use copies from every previous year in which such a magazine was published. This use of the literary magazine also can serve as motivation for budding authors and artists.

Here are a few examples of stories which children enjoy. The first was written by an eighth grader, Mr. Evan Huss.

The Strange Adventure

Billy Porter was waiting impatiently for his father. Billy had asked his father all week for an astronaut set. As the minutes went by, Billy finally said, "What's keeping him?" Just then his father came out.

"Did you buy it Dad, did ya?" Billy asked.

"I'm sorry, Billy," he said, "They sold the last set."

"Oh no! Now how am I going to play astronaut?" Billy asked disappointedly.

"You don't need all that junk to play astronaut," his father said. "Why don't you just use your imagination?"

"What's an imagination?" Billy asked.

"Your imagination is like—well, it's sort of like a thought," his father said.

"What do you mean?" Billy asked.

"You see that tree over there?" his father asked. "Well, make believe it's a knight in armor."

"That's stupid. Anyone knows it's just a dumb old maple tree," Billy said.

"Make believe it's not a tree. If you use your imagination hard enough it may seem real," his father said.

Later, Billy saw his father's old jacket.

"I know what this can be," he muttered to himself. "This will be my spacesuit." He put it on.

"Now I need a spacegun to protect me." He looked around and found a small, gunlike shaped stick on the ground.

"This can be my spacegun."

"Now comes the important thing. I need a spaceship." He thought and thought for awhile.

"I've got it!" He ran across the street into the woods and started looking for a large tree. In a minute he found one and climbed up and sat on a large branch.

"Wow, this will be a neat spaceship," he said. "Begin countdown!" he said into a twig microphone. "Ten, nine, eight, seven, six, five—what comes before five?" he thought. "Oh! Four . . . three . . . two . . . one . . . Blast off!" Billy found himself in a spacecraft shooting into space.

Billy looked out his spacecraft window just in time to see the planet Earth slowly disappear behind him. Billy was so excited he started to fiddle with the controls and switches. The ship amazingly responded with a quick turn and headed in the opposite direction. Billy then saw a kind of speedometer. It said his ship was going 2,500 miles an hour and was rising steadily.

"If only I knew how to operate this thing," he said to himself. Since he was sort of scared, Billy pushed a dark brown knot hole hoping it would bring him back to earth. But instead the mysterious craft changed course and was headed straight for another planet. Billy then looked at his speedometer, and saw 7,250 miles an hour. The planet now was getting closer and Billy knew he had to slow down or crash. He looked around and found a blinking light which said "retro-rockets." He jammed down the button and checked the speedometer. Instead of slowing down, he found himself gaining speed. The speedometer now read 12,300 miles. The planet was so close. Billy was frightened. He closed his eyes and prepared to crash. Just then a familiar voice said "Hi, Billy! Watcha doing?"

"Take me to your leader," Billy said, still not realizing where he was.

"Wad ya say, Billy?" the voice asked. Billy opened his eyes, and found himself in a huge tree with a funny looking stick in his hand.

He looked around and down the tree. Who was there but his good friend, Johnny Mitchell. Billy then realized where he was.

"Do ya feel alright?" Johnny asked.

"Sure, I feel alright," he said.

"Your mother wants you home for supper." Billy ran home, into the kitchen, and sat at the table. His mother put the food on the table.

"Billy, what did you do today?" she asked.

"Mom, if I told you, you'd *never* believe me."

The idea of space travel has certainly taken hold of our young people. The following story was written by ninth grader Deborah Trentalange.

The Explorer

My wish came true; I was the first to set foot on this new world, this new civilization.

All my life I wanted to travel into space to see a new world that existed among the stars. I would sit and gaze through my telescope for hours and see far out into space. It thrilled me to think that someday I might be the first woman to set out into the vast wilderness that lay ahead. No one had ever set foot on another planet; it was something strange to everyone. So my career started. I went to all the possible schools that a future astronaut could attend. By the time I was old enough to even think of entering into a spaceship, they had perfected the long dreamed of ship that might do the trick . . . the ship that could possibly reach another planet. Would it be possible that I would be the astronaut to be picked to go? The day came. There were ten of us from which to choose. Being the only woman, it had never dawned on me I would have a chance to be chosen. But I was. I was not sure whether I wanted to go now or not, whether I wanted to discover this other world. I was not sure I wanted to find out what there was to discover, but my chance came, so I took it.

Time was short and finally the moment came when I set my foot into the spaceship that would carry me to one of the planets that has bewildered my civilization since it began . . . 3, 2, 1! Off through the stars I traveled on and on, closer and closer. Then the moment came; I would now ride down low enough to examine this new world that has long waited to be discovered. Down lower and lower till I could see life, unchanged from that of mine . . . buildings, vehicles, roads, all the same! I was first from my planet to set foot on EARTH!

Book Reporting with a Difference

Instead of doing formal book reporting, there are a number of methods which can be used which your children will enjoy.

1. Have them design a book jacket and write a blurb to accompany it. They can study existing book jackets (on teenage or young adult books) for samples. Encourage them to be creative.

2. Allow children to review the book for a newspaper. Have the youngsters read several reviews to be found in publications of his or her own grade level. A review would include things the reader liked, things he or she didn't like, possibly one or two exciting parts. However, it would not give away the story, and, particularly, the ending. If your class is publishing its own newspaper or magazine, book reviews should play an important part, and certainly more than one or two may be used.

One class did an entire newspaper of reviews—books, records, films, television programs. Each youngster did his or her own thing. There were two requirements—the piece had to be well written, and no two reviews were of the same material.

3. Have those inclined to do so create a series of cartoons or illustrations for the story. They should be prepared to describe these to the class.

4. Have several children read the same book and then, working as a group, create and act out a play from one or two parts of it. (Specifically avoid doing a play from a whole book. Far too difficult.)

5. Have children "interview" a character from the book; as they do the dialogue have them figure out how the person would react, and what he would say.

6. Suggest children select the most humorous incident, and prepare to read it to the class.

7. Tell the children to write a short summary of the book, but to substitute another ending. This can be great fun, and sometimes very interesting. If you find your children's responses are good, have them read to the class aloud.

8. Ask the child to select 25 new words from the story, look up the definitions and present them to the class. They should include sentences relevant to the story.

9. The most original method of book reporting we have encountered was developed by Mr. Robert Pisano, some of whose other techniques are also included in these pages.

"When we've finished a book I find the young adults I teach enjoy writing acrostics," he said. Acrostics are poems written using a particular word as a basis. The word is written down a page, one letter per line vertically. Then each letter is used as the first word of a line.

For example, from the novel and then television play, *Lisa, Bright and Dark,* by John Neufeld, the student used the words SAD LISA.

The result:

S adness in her life so soon
A nd wishing someone would care.
D ying emotions, brightness dulled.
L ying on her bed in her own world.
I f someone would help, understand.
S ympathy to her, love for her once but
A fter all, it's no use now she's dead!

The next three are written about the young hero (really anti-hero) of *Catcher in the Rye*, Holden Caulfield, and are given to show the young people's train of thought about him.

H e is a strange boy in many ways.
O ver and over he dreams strange dreams
L ies are an important part of his life.
D umb is the way he is in school.
E very time he doesn't like you he says you are phony
N ot too many people are good in his mind.

H olden Caulfield. A lonely boy.
O nly his sister
L oves him.
D eserted and alone he's
E ntirely confused about life.
N ot knowing where to begin.

H is only friend is Phoebe
O n to other Places
L iving alone and thinking
D eciding to go home
E ven though he tried
N ever to go back to school again.

Incidentally, try this method of writing poems yourself. We've found it's really much easier than any other method. The letters serve as guidelines—almost push you along.

Follow the Author

Encourage your children to "follow the author." If they discover a book they particularly enjoy, they should read more of the same author's works. We recall, personally, doing this with Zane Gray. Girls enjoy the Nancy Drew series, and younger children the Dr. Doolittle stories. Even adults are devotees of authors, such as Mary Renault, or Ernest K. Gann.

See the Movie—Read the Book, or
Read the Book—See the Movie

One seventh grade class, after being taken to see Scrooge, was very anxious to read the original work, even though the Christmas holidays had come and gone. More current literature has the same effect; the order of viewing and reading, or vice versa doesn't seem to matter. We found this technique very fine when the eighth grade read *Julius Caesar*. We still believe that our young adults, at that level, can get a great deal from reading Shakespeare, particularly if the reading is either preceded or followed by seeing a movie or play production of it.

For children with a short attention span, to make reading fun, anthologies are better than novels. An excellent example for seventh and eighth graders is *Live Stories*, Vol. I and II, published by the New York City Board of Education, and available at $1 each. This particular anthology contains seven basic categories which follow:

Our American Way of Life

Family Album

Sports and Hobbies

Love is a Many-Splendored Thing

Dating and Mating

The Ladder of Ambition

Values and Ideals

These categories, as you can see, take into consideration the children's interests. Choose anthologies which do so.

In addition to this, your stories should contain material to which the children can personally relate. Imagine a young boy reading "Runt, A Gridiron He-Man," or a young lady, "A Gift of Love."

Comic Books, and Mad Magazine

If we want our youngsters to read, we have to begin at their level—but often their level is somewhere in never-never land. Never read books, anyway! How about comic books or *Mad* magazine? We've seen children who would never turn to a book for entertainment literally devour *Mad* magazine. While we cannot possibly subscribe to everything in it, we do think if it gets particular children to read, why not use it?

Reading Races

We personally saw one child read more than 160 books while she was in the sixth grade of elementary school. Why? Because her class was involved in a reading race. A huge poster was placed on the back wall of the classroom, and each time a child finished a book, and gave a very short report on it, he or she would paste an indicator on the chart. These indicators were small flags, and the color used depended on the subject read.

This method, used by Mrs. Florence Hampton, was extremely effective.

"I'd rather read than watch television," was the youngster's comment at the time.

Reading to Do Projects

If children need to read in order to enable them to do something they really want to do, they'll learn more about reading than all of the coaxing and cajoling we can do.

With children who are "turned off" in respect to reading, try to find something. It may be photography, or playing a guitar, building a rocket, or putting together a radio. If you can discover an interest, you can capitalize on it.

This type of learning can seem to be almost a miracle. We saw a child raise his reading level by three years because of an interest he developed in film making, for example. When the ability to read is needed, this is an entirely different story from just reading because the teacher asks you to.

If no other method has worked with a particular child, try this one. You may have to play detective to find his interests, but if you can, perhaps you can produce a miracle!

If bread is the staff of life nutritionally, reading is in that position intellectually. Do all you can to make it a pleasure rather than a duty, and you will be enriching your children's lives not only today, but forever.

SUMMARY

If you can wage a successful campaign to make reading fun for your pupils, you will have a permanent positive effect on your children's lives—not only today, but for their entire future. In this chapter you read of techniques which have met with great success. Begin by taking every child you teach to the library in your school, and to the public library, as well. Make these trips pleasant, and get the children to associate the library and reading with pleasure, and with good experiences. Establish a book and magazine corner in your room, for reading after work is completed. In your lesson plans allot time for pleasure reading. Form class book clubs and use unusual methods for having the children report on books they've read. Use television scripts to encourage reading, and utilize the technique of "See the movie—read the book," or "Read the book—see the movie." Teach your children how to "follow an author." Use projects to entice your youngsters to read.

Inculcating a love of reading is an aim well worth your efforts, for, if a child never discovers the pleasures reading can bring, he or she will miss out on a great deal of the enjoyment life has to offer.

13

Activities for Teaching Love of Our Country

As with every subject, but particularly with this one, "love of country," it is the teacher's enthusiasm and verve which will make it succeed or fail. "Love of country" is a subject we're afraid has been largely ignored, of late. The era we are living through has been almost one of constant negative criticism (justifiably so), but it is our very strong feeling that this should be changed beginning today, and beginning in our classrooms. We certainly agree there is much to criticize, but that, nevertheless, this is the greatest country on earth—and we are tremendously fortunate to be American citizens.

As a student of American history, you have learned of past periods which had tremendous problems. These problems may not appear now to have been as severe as ours of today. However, the "Great Depression" was certainly an extremely grave time, with people's life savings being wiped out almost overnight, and thousands unable to earn a living. The suicide rate was astounding, with men throwing themselves out of windows or off roofs of office buildings because of events over which they had absolutely no control. As bad as Watergate seems, it doesn't compare to the sadness of those days. But even the problems of 1929 to 1933 were ultimately solved, and the nation and its people moved ahead. We cannot let the difficulties of the last ten or twenty years defeat us. As long as we are not engaged in war, there should be nothing to faze us. The proverb "This, too, shall pass," says it all. Administrators and administrations will change, and we will elect new leaders. Realize though that what is so great about this nation is that we have a system of government established two hundred years ago which still meets our complex needs today as well as it met them then. We have the instruments for continual improvement within our grasp.

If you are one of those young people who was, and is being "turned off" by the history of the past decade, we implore you to read this chapter. Give it a chance to percolate in your brain, because we honestly believe, if you care about people, you must realize just how much this "experiment in democracy" has done to help the poor person, the ones who begged and starved years ago, and, indeed, are starving today in many parts of the world. We have our freedoms, here, guaranteed by that truly miraculous document, the Constitution, and particularly by the Bill of Rights. We agree we have a long way to go, but look how far we've come—in terms of our own history, and in terms of the world.

We do not ask you to teach the glorification of wars. You will note in this chapter, we have scrupulously avoided even discussing them. Our purpose is to teach a belief in our people and in our Constitution.

Elementary school teachers have a rare opportunity to reach their children. If you're the type of teacher we believe you are (one reason being because you are taking the time to read this book), we know your children love you—and loving you they will take heed of what you teach them. It's really of utmost importance that you teach them to love all of mankind, and to love their country.

The idea for this chapter came from a record which we heard broadcast by a famous disc-jockey, "Murray the K." Hardly his style of record, he nevertheless introduced it, and its popularity is growing tremendously. However, the real punch line is to be found in the article from *The New York Times* of Sunday, January 13, 1974.

Gordon Sinclair

CANADIAN RECORD HAILING U.S. A HIT

Journalist Tired of Hearing Americans 'Kicked Around'

By WILLIAM BORDERS
Special to The New York Times

TORONTO, Jan. 9 — Gordon Sinclair, a Toronto radio commentator who is "damned tired of seeing the Americans get kicked around," recently broadcast an editorial saying so, and now finds himself something of a hero.

His narration, defending the Americans as "the most generous and possibly the least appreciated people in all the earth," has been reprinted in dozens of American newspapers, and a recording of it titled "Americans" has become one of the fastest-selling records in the United States.

With sales of two million in the four weeks since its release, the record has climbed to No. 8 on one American popularity chart and No. 13 on another, putting the genial 73-year-old Canadian journalist in the unaccustomed company of rock bands and pop singers.

"I guess I hit a nerve, praising the people down there when they weren't expecting it," Mr. Sinclair said, as he sat in his comfortable suburban home, sorting through some of the 50,000 letters of thanks that Americans have written him since last June, when he broadcast his composition on Station CRFB here.

He had seen flooding in the Mississippi River valley on television that morning, he recalls, and was impressed that the American farmers whose crops had been ruined "weren't whining about it."

"I can name you 5,000 times when the Americans raced to the aid of other people in trouble," he declared in one of the most quoted sections of his four-minute narration. "Can you name me even one time when someone else raced to the Americans in trouble?"

"When distant cities are hit by earthquakes, it is the United States that hurries in to help. So far this spring 59 American communities have been flattened by tornadoes. Nobody has helped."

The record, reviewing how United States aid revitalized the world after World War II and pointing out that no other nation could "even consider" putting a man on the moon, then alludes to the national trauma of the Watergate affair:

"You talk about scandals and the Americans put theirs right in the store window for everybody to look at. They will come out of this thing with their flag high. And when they do, they are entitled to thumb their nose at the lands that are gloating over their present troubles."

Mr. Sinclair has made a recording of this editorial, with "The Battle Hymn of the Republic" in the background. The version that is selling best is by Byron MacGregor, a 25-year-old radio announcer from Windsor, Ont., who reads it over a background of "America the Beautiful."

Next: Gettysburg Address

"Mine is exactly the same words, but it's faster than Sinclair's, more upbeat," explained Mr. MacGregor, who had never made a record before but is now planning to record the Gettysburg Address.

In accordance with Mr. Sinclair's desire, neither man has made any money on "Americans"; the royalties, which Mr. MacGregor already put at more than $100,000 in his case, are being donated to the American Red Cross.

"I'm an old man, and I don't need the money," explained Mr. Sinclair, a former foreign correspondent for The Toronto Star.

Many Americans are grateful for the gesture.

"It is not very often we Americans read something complimentary about our country," a woman in New Kensington, Pa., wrote.

"Yours is the first tribute that I have ever heard," wrote a man in Madison, Wis. "It is a warm feeling."

Princess Grace of Monaco sent a note of appreciation, and so did a young seaman serving in the Atlantic. And in the kind of greeting Mr. Sinclair particularly cherishes, a man in Indiana wrote on the back of a Christmas card: "God bless you, neighbor."

The text which follows—which was read to a musical background on the record—was distributed, free, by Radio Station WHN in New York:

GORDON SINCLAIR

LET'S BE PERSONAL broadcast of June 5th, 1973

Topic: *Americans*

The United States dollar took another pounding on German, French and British exchanges this morning, hitting the lowest point ever known in West Germany. It has declined there by 41% since 1971 and this Canadian thinks it is time to speak up for the Americans as the most generous and possibly the least-appreciated people in all the earth.

As long as sixty years ago, when I first started to read newspapers, I read of floods on the Yellow River and the Yangtze. Who rushed in with men and money to help? The Americans did.

They have helped control floods on the Nile, the Amazon, the Ganges and the Niger. Today, the rich bottomland of the Mississippi is under water and no foreign land has sent a dollar to help. Germany, Japan and, to a lesser extent, Britain and Italy, were lifted out of the debris of war by the Americans who poured in billions of dollars and forgave other billions in debts. None of these countries is today paying even the interest on its remaining debts to the United States.

When the franc was in danger of collapsing in 1956, it was the Americans who propped it up and their reward was to be insulted and swindled on the streets of Paris. I was there. I saw it.

When distant cities are hit by earthquake, it is the United States that hurries in to help . . . Managua, Nicaragua is one of the most recent examples. So far this spring, 59 American communities have been flattened by tornadoes. Nobody has helped.

The Marshall Plan . . . the Truman Policy . . . all pumped billions upon billions of dollars into discouraged countries. Now newspapers in those countries are writing about the decadent war-mongering Americans. I'd like to see just one of those countries that is gloating over the erosion of the United States dollar build its own airplanes.

Come on . . . let's hear it! Does any other country in the world have a plane to equal the Boeing Jumbo Jet, the Lockheed Tristar or the Douglas 10? If so, why don't they fly them? Why do all international lines except Russia fly American planes? Why does no other land on earth even *consider* putting a man or woman on the moon?

You talk about Japanese technocracy and you get radios. You talk about German technocracy and you get automobiles. You talk about American technocracy and you find men on the moon, not once, but several times . . . and safely home again. You talk about scandals and the Americans put theirs right in the store window for everybody to look at. Even the draft dodgers are not pursued and hounded. They are here on our streets, most of them . . . unless they are breaking Canadian laws . . . are getting American dollars from Ma and Pa at home to spend here.

When the Americans get out of this bind . . . as they will . . . who could blame them if they said "the Hell with the rest of the world"? Let someone *else* buy the Israel bonds. Let someone else build or repair foreign dams or design foreign buildings that won't shake apart in earthquakes.

When the railways of France, Germany and India were breaking down through age, it was the Americans who rebuilt them. When the Pennsylvania Railroad and the New York Central went broke, nobody loaned them an old caboose. Both are *still* broke. I can name to you 5,000 times when the Americans raced to the help of other people in trouble.

Can you name me even *one* time when someone else raced to the Americans in trouble? I don't think there was outside help even during the San Francisco earthquake.

Our neighbors have faced it alone and I'm one Canadian who is damned tired of hearing them kicked around. They will come out of this thing with their flag high. And when they do, they are entitled to thumb their nose at the lands that are gloating over their present troubles.

I hope Canada is not one of these. But there are many smug, self-righteous Canadians. And finally, the American Red Cross was told at its 48th Annual Meeting in New Orleans this morning that it was broke.

This year's disasters . . . with the year less than half over . . . has taken it all and nobody . . . but nobody . . . has helped.

What can you do with this record? Of course, play it for your children. Then go over the words, and discuss them—so that the youngsters understand all of them. You may wish to read the article to the class, too, so that they understand the type of man Mr. Gordon Sinclair is. You may have the children do dramatic readings themselves—individually or as a choral group. You can have the words printed and posted in your classroom. Emphasize the fact that Mr. Sinclair is a Canadian, not an American.

The Pledge of Allegiance

One of the ways we make our children conscious of their heritage is by saying the Pledge of Allegiance. How can we make that more meaningful?

We teach the Pledge to our youngsters when they're very young. Far too often they don't understand the words they are saying, or they get them a bit garbled. An example is the youngster who pledged allegiance to the "republicans," and to "Richard Sands." We never quite figured out just whom he thought Richard Sands was, or why he was pledging allegiance to him. Of course, "republicans" refers to "republic" and the next phrase is "for which it stands," not "Richard Sands."

With every class you teach, go over the meaning of the words "pledge," "allegiance," "republic," "indivisible," "liberty," and "justice." Our children should understand them! They're important words—and almost a summary of what our democracy is all about.

Trips

We've already mentioned taking trips in an earlier chapter. However, it bears repetition here, because there are so many places which instill a tremendous sense of history when they are visited.

If you can take your children to Washington, D.C., do so by all means! Many, many youngsters never get there if they are not taken by their schools. To get the maximum benefits from this trip, prepare for it in advance. Discuss with the children what they will see and what took place, and takes place, there. You can divide your class into committees. Have one study the White House, another the Capital, others can cover the monuments, the Pentagon, and the office buildings, and the museums. If you have the time, and can include a trip to Mount Vernon, do so, by all means.

In studying each place, encourage the children to bring in people. The rotunda of the Capital, for instance, is the spot where John Kennedy lay in state after his death, and where thousands of people viewed his body. Perhaps some of the children's families recall seeing this on television.

You will need parents to travel with your group for security reasons. If you have enough adults to feel safe, we suggest you take the children to the Lincoln Memorial at ten or so in the evening. (If you can visit the Ford theatre before, do so.) But late at night, when the memorial is quiet, seeing it is, to this author, one of the most emotionally stirring sights in the entire world. Much of this is lost if you go there with hundreds of people milling around. But devoid of visitors, the Daniel Chester French statute seems lifelike (in spite of its size) and you feel a closeness to Lincoln which is quite unbelievable.

Washington is a magnificent city, with beautiful buildings, and the Capital dominating the whole area. It will, with your help, really inspire your children.

A trip to Philadelphia can provide another wonderful experience for your children. On such a visit we saw one child place his hands lovingly on the Liberty Bell, then turn to another and say, "I touched it. I touched it. I really touched it." Independence Hall is an inspiration, if you make it so.

The origins of our way of life can be seen in many places—such as Williamsburg, Va., and Jamestown; or Plymouth and Salem, Mass. The growth of the nation, as people spread out in all directions, can be seen in many localities, often marked by National Historic Sites. The humble birthplaces of some of our presidents are often commemorated, showing they were human beings, just as each one of us is.

This nation was the first nation to guarantee religious freedom. Indeed, religious people have done a great deal to foster its growth. The state of California grew because of the chain of missions established in a line from San Diego in the South to Sonoma in the North. The missions were one day's walk apart, and were responsible for the early development of the area.

In the East, you can show your children the Amish people living a very different life from most of us, and guaranteed the right to live it by the Constitution.

If you take your class on trips, be dramatic as you discuss the reasons for the trip. Show them why the place is special, and in what way it has contributed to this nation.

Another trip we would like to suggest is to the Hall of Presidents at Disney World, Lake Buena Vista (Near Orlando), Florida. If you have the opportunity, take your children to this particular attraction. In a short time it gives the youngsters an understanding of some of our most important history.

Reading to Inspire Patriotism

Recently we read a short version of the famous classic "The Last Day." It had appeared in *Table Talk*, a four-page treat published by the Marriott Corporation, and was written by the editor, Mr. Martin Buxbaum, who graciously gave us permission to reprint it.

We suggest you read it aloud to your children. Then *don't discuss it*. Ask the girls and boys to think about it. Here's the story:

> We humans never know how deep our love is for anything until we lose what we have loved. When a man loses his wife, for example, or a wife her husband, it is at the very moment of loss that the *true* depth of their love becomes known.
>
> When I was very young, I came across a small book which had been translated from the original French edition. It was published in 1922 or thereabouts. The book disappeared long ago, but one short story from it remains in my memory—perhaps because of the great lesson it contained:

> ### The Last Day

> Little Pierre was again late for school. He could never resist stopping along the way if he saw something interesting—and he *always* saw something interesting. Today, it was a cat stalking a pigeon. The cat crouched, eyes staring at every move the pigeon made, tail twitching ever so slightly. Slowly, the cat moved one foot forward at a time, and then—just as the cat was about to pounce, a *man* walked around the corner. Frightened, the pigeon flew away with a soft whistle of its wings. The cat sat back on its haunches and stared upward. Pierre laughed.
>
> When Pierre came into the small schoolroom, he took off his beret and slipped into his seat with one smooth, familiar motion. There he sat, hands folded on the desk, waiting for his teacher to scold him.
>
> This morning, however, the teacher just stood, a solemn look on his face. The class was curiously quiet. Pierre noted that some of the children were crying.
>
> "For your benefit, my little Pierre," said the teacher, softly, "I will repeat what I have already told the class.

"I have been notified by the German authorities that our beloved Alsace-Lorraine has been taken over by German troops. You children are not to be taught French any longer. All French books and flags will be replaced with German books and German flags. Tomorrow, you will have a German teacher. But for this last day, we can *still be French!*"

Pierre was stunned. He thought back of the many times when he'd failed to do his lessons, or had been late for school. How he *wished* he could recall those days and the days when he had pretended to be sick and stayed home! Now, suddenly, he realized how very much his country meant to him.

No group ever studied harder than Pierre and his friends on the last day. It was if they were trying to compress a lifetime of French education into a few short hours.

The end of the school day finally came. The teacher spoke:

"The hour has come, my children. Please leave your books on the desk." And then it was as if he began to think aloud. "What shall I give to each of you? What *one* thought can I leave with you, even if you forgot everything else I have taught you?"

The Tricolor of France stood in the corner. Walking over to it slowly, he carefully removed it from its staff and held it out in front of him. "Look well upon this, my beloved countrymen. It is your flag and mine. Remember to always keep it in your hearts, for there, no one can ever take it away from you. As long as this flag remains in your hearts, France will live! *Vive la France!*"

* * * * *

I have seen our beloved Stars and Stripes torn down from its mast and burned. But remembering the story of Pierre, I knew that if every American flag in our nation were to be destroyed tomorrow, it would still live, for there are too many of us who would keep it always in our hearts.

Another of Mr. Buxbaum's pieces which we treasure (we personally made a dozen photocopies because we were so afraid of losing it) follows. Again, we suggest you read it to your children, and then simply ask them to think about it. Of course, if you feel they will get more out of it by discussing it, please, please do so.

What Will They Be Remembered For?

This year is again a key election year—a year of destiny for the men who will be chosen for the highest public offices in the land.

With our votes we will make our selections of these leaders, based upon faith that they *will* represent us—wisely and well, honestly and unselfishly. Therefore, when we read in the newspapers of an elected official betraying our trust by sacrificing honor for greed, we are profoundly shocked.

During the past 196 years, we have had many greats among our elected leaders, but few who have made the sacrifices which were made by the signers of the Declaration of Independence. Their absolute faith in their cause, their honesty, courage, and adherence to principle, will remain as perpetual examples to all who hold public office.

On July 4, 1776, the Continental Congress of the United States approved Thomas Jefferson's draft of the Declaration of Independence. It was signed by 56 members. These 56 came from all walks of life—scholars and farmers, the elegant and the plain, the rich and those we would now term middle-class. And as these members penned their signatures—some carefully and methodically, some strong and bold, and some with graceful flourish, many thoughts must have run through their minds. They well knew that this was no idle declaration—that in the eyes of the Crown, it was a direct act of treason and would be dealt with as such.

Each man knew that he was signing away the safety and security of his family, all of his possessions, and possibly his life—yet each man signed without hesitation.

British retaliation came—swiftly, as they knew it would. The interior of George Clymer's spacious house was literally ripped apart by Hessian troops . . . Francis Hopkinson and his family were forced from their home at bayonet point . . . Thomas McKean and his family moved five times to escape persecution . . . Lewis Morris had a 3,000-acre estate. The British set fire to 1,000 acres of woods around it and then destroyed everything in the fine manor house . . . John Hart (Honest John) saw his grist mill and his sawmill burned, along with his 400-acre farm. He and his 13 children were forced to run for their lives.

Nine signers of the Declaration died of wounds or hardships; another five were imprisoned and in some cases given unbelievably brutal treatment. Many wives, sons and daughters of the signers were either killed, jailed or persecuted. The houses of 12 of the signers were burned to the ground. *And yet—any one of these men could have turned back at any time he chose.* Each of them was offered immunity, rewards of money, restoration of their homes, release of their loved ones and a position with the Crown if they would but switch their allegiance. *History records with pride that not a single man did.* Their individual honor, like their new nation, remained intact.

The people of this new United States of America watched these men—their leaders. The people drew courage from *their* courage, and faith from *their* faith. Had any of these signers been less courageous, less honest, or less principled, the whole cause of freedom might have been lost.

These 56 men are long dead but this is not important, for all men die. What *is* important is that they were willing to give up everything precious to them for the sake of their people and their country. For this these leaders will be remembered as long as there *is* a United States of America.

The men who hold public office today, and those who will . . . hold office in the months and years ahead—how many of *these* will be remembered when history is written? And if they *are* remembered, for *what* will they be remembered?

A Nation of Immigrants

The heading above is, of course, the title of a fine book by Franklin D. Roosevelt. We are, almost every one of us, descended from immigrants. The important point for our children to learn is why their families came here. To motivate the unit, read Emma Lazarus' fine lines to them—just as they appear on the Statue of Liberty:

Give me your tired, your poor
Your huddled masses yearning to breathe free,
The wretched refuse of your teeming shore.
Send these, the homeless, tempest-tost to me,
I lift my lamp beside the golden door!

We suggest you have your youngsters interview their parents, or preferably their grandparents, to find out their personal reasons for emigrating to the United States. If the youngsters seem reluctant to speak, you can have them write their findings anonymously, and then have the papers read aloud. Even today people come to this country for greater opportunity and for the freedoms we offer. You can, if you wish, contrast this with news reports of happenings in other nations.

Who Are Your Three Favorite Presidents?

You may wish to have your children do a research paper to find out who their three favorite presidents are—and why. (Including three makes this far more of a challenge than just one or two—because they must choose one more than Lincoln and Washington.) Stress the fact that the reasons are the most important aspect.

Make Big Celebrations

Our 200th birthday is, of course, cause for a most celebrated occasion. But why not celebrate other nationally historic events with equal verve? Making our children conscious of the important events through fun and through new ideas can have a very positive effect on them. Oh, we all know about George Washington and the cherry tree—but that's become a cliché, and so overworked! There's so much about our first president which is truly spectacular. For example, had he but accepted he would have been crowned king. A personally very ambitious man, yet he refused! Our founding fathers were human beings—but great! Help your children to see this. We've often tended to overplay one aspect, such as Lincoln's log cabin, and lose so much else! Do some research yourself as well as having the children do it. We know you'll be richer for it, and so will the youngsters.

Essay Contests

Recently our children were asked to write essays on the topic "A Child of 1774." The results were very fine. Many children really got into the subject—quite involved in it. They were asked to compare the children's lives then and now.

Children enjoy contests, and, with this as motivation, we've found the response excellent.

Recommending Television Programs

Often there are television programs being shown which are wonderful lessons in love of country. For example, Texaco presented "Trial by Fire," an excellent program about Lincoln and General

McClellan. Even though it involved war, this was worthwhile for young people to see.

Find out, in advance, which programs will be shown. A review of the Sunday newspaper will often give you much information in advance. *Scholastic*'s teacher edition lists programs a month ahead —which is even better, and it gives you teaching guides, too.

You can suggest pupils see the programs, or give viewing them as assignments. (Be sure, in that case, that everyone in the class has access to a television set.) It's possible, too, to give bonuses for watching a program and writing a short review of it. (The 5 W's—"who, what, when, where, why" is sufficient.)

Kinescopes or Video-taping

As we said, recently there have been a number of superb programs done for television. One was Hallmark's story of George Washington called "The World Turned Upside Down." (The title is from an old folk song.) Video-taping the program makes it available for replaying any time it's wanted. If you don't have the equipment, it is possible to ask to borrow the kinescope.

Making a library of such television offerings can be extremely worthwhile. For a nominal sum any program can be taped. The initial expenditure for the equipment is high—but perhaps your PTA can help you to obtain it.

Studying the History of Your Area

There is lots of fascinating history right in your own back yard. Have your children learn about it—with you. Is there a local museum to visit, and in which to study? Are there senior citizens willing to speak to your class, telling them about people and places they remember? Are there old records in the archives, waiting to be read? Is there a City Hall with lots of interesting information?

You can involve your youngsters in a project researching your area which can encompass social studies and language arts very effectively. Music and art can be added. Then bring in those interviews mentioned previously. Perhaps you want to combine all of the material in a class newspaper or magazine. The possibilities are endless. Your children can make dioramas, or do murals, montages or even photographic essays.

Remember, as they do this, to strengthen their positive feelings for our beautiful land.

Pick Your Personal Hero

Another topic you may choose is to have each child select his or her own personal hero, and then to learn as much as he or she can about that person. Mention that this person does not have to be dead. He or she can be very much alive. It is unusual for a child to select a person who is not an American, but if they do, that's alright, too.

Give the children time to select their person.

My personal hero is Thomas Jefferson. Most people will tend to select Abraham Lincoln. For years Franklin D. Roosevelt was very popular, but he seems to be losing his position. Eleanor Roosevelt, too, made her mark on people's emotions. So have the astronauts.

The *World Book Encyclopedia* is good for browsing, and for "shopping."

Encourage the children to think carefully about this. You may hold a series of "introductions," during which you discuss some information about each person. *Bring in some women, as well as men, and, of course, be sure to include individuals of all races, creeds and colors.*

An assignment of this type, if the children are motivated, can teach them a great deal more about history, current events and love of country then merely studying an era or period.

Using Music and Poetry for Teaching
Love of Country

Have you heard the superb "Ballad for Americans" done by the Johnny Mann Singers? It's just one example of a song which can instill the emotions we are looking to instill. And so can "God Bless America," if your children have not been subjected to it too often. (Remember, even if you have, they may not have been.) "The House I Live In" is another example. There are literally dozens of songs which tell of the nation's growth, its trials and tribulations. Again we must mention that we do not mean war songs, with one exception—"The Battle Hymn of the Republic." This we must mention because of its tremendous depth and meaning. Earlier in this book you read about the excellent use made of the song "America the Beautiful." Which songs make you react emotionally? These are the ones to play for your children.

Many people were taught "In Flanders Field the poppies grow" but here again we get involved with war—something we ask you to avoid. But consider "Oh Captain, My Captain," written by Walt Whitman to express his great sadness at the death of Abraham Lincoln. Many of Whitman's poems sing of his love of America. Tune in to this type of material and use it judiciously.

How Can We Improve Our Country?

At no point should you ever maintain that our nation is perfect. How could it be—when we are over two hundred million people, working and living together? But if we can all try for improvements, they are certain possible.

Far too much time of late has been spent by the media, by the Congress, by the people, in discussing what has gone wrong. If we can shift the emphasis to what is right, and, more importantly, *what we can do*, then we are in a position to accomplish great things. One young school teacher realized the desperate need for a playground in her community. She found an empty lot, and convinced the owner of the need for the playground. He leased it for $1 per year. An insurance company agreed to insure it gratis. A local bank contributed the equipment. The people living in the area donated their time and their labor. Instead of complaining about the lack of a playground, this young woman did something about it. Eleanor Roosevelt is often quoted as having said, "It is better to light a single candle than to curse the darkness." So it should be with us. Even young children can participate in activities such as the collection of newspapers or aluminum cans. They can work to clean up their neighborhoods.

Teach your children to be positive, rather than negative, to build up rather than to tear down, to improve conditions rather than to bemoan them. This, to us, is what love of country really is—a desire to help the people who make up this nation, followed by positive action.

Photographic Essays, Montages and Drawings

Your children will enjoy taking photographs. It is one of the most gratifying types of activity, and you can use this most effectively to teach love of country. Some of the topics you can use are photographic essays of people or places, of progress, of items of historic significance.

Montages are very rewarding, and can be done at far less expense. We saw one of "America the Beautiful" which combined people with places. It was magnificent, and showed a great deal of love which the children managed to put into it. The same basic design can be used with art work of all kinds—murals, paintings, designs.

Talk About Your Feelings, and What It Means to Be an AMERICAN

We have discovered that many people are painfully ignorant about the true meaning of being an American—with a very sparce knowledge of their own country's history and background. Talk about the subject! Don't be afraid to mention it, and to show your emotions. One wonders why anyone should be reluctant to say, "I love this country."

It would be ridiculous to refuse to admit we have serious problems. The times we are living through are, indeed, difficult ones. But it is important for your children to see the assets this country has to offer. The Constitution protects us—as no document has ever protected the individuals of any nation before. Many others have copied it. We have already discussed the value of teaching what the freedoms we are guaranteed really mean. Every child should have an understanding of this. Hopefully there will be no more wars which make it necessary for our young men to die for it, but all of us should be willing to live and work for it.

SUMMARY

In this chapter we have discussed a number of techniques for teaching what we consider to be the most important subject we have to offer—love of our country. These include using songs and recordings, trips, readings, research and celebrations. Television has much fine material to offer, in this regard, too.

We believe that the best possible way we can show our love of our country is by taking positive steps to improve it, and teaching our children to do the same.

John F. Kennedy's quotation is worth putting up on your wall: "Ask not what your country can do for you, but what you can do for your country." Every single living thing, plant, animal, city and state consists of two basic processes—building up and breaking down. Let's make sure the emphasis is on the building up!

INDEX